JERUSALEM
The Home in Our Hearts

JERUSALEM
The Home in Our Hearts

A Family's Multigenerational Story of Faith, Hope, and Resilience

Saliba Sarsar

Holy Land Books
An imprint of Noble Book Publishing Incorporated
N. Bethesda, MD

© 2018 by Saliba Sarsar. All rights reserved. Except for brief quotations in critical publications or reviews, no part of this book may be reproduced in any manner without written permission from the publisher.

Hania Sarsar, my youngest daughter, designed the book cover.

Christine Kattan, my niece, took the photo of the front cover. It shows Jabal Sahyoun or Mount Zion in Jerusalem, which is north of Abu Tor/Al-Thawri. It is the location of King David's Tomb; the Cenacle or site of The Last Supper; Dormition Abby, where Mary, Jesus's mother, fell into eternal sleep; and a few Christian cemeteries where several family members are buried.

Imad Zakharia, my brother-in-law, took the photo of the back cover. It is of an olive tree in the Garden of Gethsemane at the foot of the Mount of Olives, and one of eight that are among the most ancient in the world. Gethsemane, meaning "oil press" in Aramaic, is where Jesus Christ prayed the night before His crucifixion.

Library of Congress Cataloging-in-Publication Date

Jerusalem: the home in our hearts / Saliba Sarsar
    236 Pages 22.86cm.
    Includes bibliographical references
    ISBN-13: 978-1-7320286-1-6 (pbk.)
    ISBN-10: 1-7320286-1-3 (pbk.)
    1. Christian Family—Multigenerational story. 2. Jerusalem—Home. 3. Russian-Greek-Palestinian background—Ethno-religious roots. 4. Al-Thawri / Abu Tor—Neighborly relations. 5. Six-Day War, June 1967—Influence. 6. Children of War—Enemies / Friends. 7. Palestinian-Israeli peace—Future prospects. I. Title.
Library of Congress Control Number: 2018952757

Holy Land Books
An imprint of Noble Book Publishing Incorporated
11200 Rockville Pike
Suite 405
N. Bethesda, MD 20852
www.noblebookpublishing.com

Printed in the United States of America

Contents

Preface: A Living Mosaic ix
1. War, 1967 1
2. Post-War Echoes 25
3. Family Roots 41
4. Parents' Wedding 63
5. Our Neighborhood, 1940s 73
6. War, 1948 87
7. Our Neighborhood, 1950-2000 101
8. Our Neighbors, Our Friends 117
9. Family Profiles 133
Afterword: Our Sacred Trust 163

Endnotes 193

Author's Biography 211

Figure
1. Sarsar Family Tree 136

Maps
1. The Old City of Jerusalem and Her Environs xiv
2. Territories Occupied by Israel in June 1967 28
3. Pre- and Post-1967 Jerusalem's Municipal Boundaries 31
4. Comparison of 1947 Partition Plan Borders and Armistice Lines of 1949 91
5. Abu Tor/Al-Thawri 130

Family Photos 171

PREFACE
A LIVING MOSAIC

Colorful tesserae—flat, rectangular,
rounded, square—flow into formation
as if by magical hands, by heart strings
reaching out to humanity and
the rest of creation. Stars, crosses,
crescents glow in spirit, on minds
dreaming, yearning for home devoid

of zealot crusaders, modern centurions, and
the deadly toys of aggression, of war.
We—the ordinary people—await another re-
creation: the power of compassion,
of love, to break the chain of hate,
of recrimination. The gifts of faith and
hope must conquer fear and discrimination.

The city of Jerusalem is my home. She is our collective home. She is where we—Palestinian Arabs (Muslim and Christian), Israelis (Jewish, Muslim, and Christian), and others—live and work against a backdrop of constant uncertainty and, at times, in less than peaceful conditions.

My own family struggled and survived in Jerusalem amidst conflict, loss, and pain. She is where I was born and raised, where I took my initial breaths and saw first light. She is where I learned the alphabet and discovered right from wrong. The seeds of my identity took root in Jerusalem. My earliest words and actions engendered meaning and significances that would later define who I am, what I believe, and what impact I may have on others.

Jerusalem is known by seventy names in biblical and post-biblical literature, including *"shalem"* (whole) or peace (Genesis 14:18), "a tumultuous city, a joyous city" (Isaiah 22:2), and "righteous dwelling" (Jeremiah 31:22). Arabs and Muslims call her *al-Quds* ("the holy"), and most Israeli Jews and Jews in the Diaspora call her *Yerushalayim* ("the abode of peace"). Reflecting on their experiences in Jerusalem, some authors have called her the "torn city,"[1] "city of mirrors,"[2] "city of stone,"[3] "contested city,"[4] "divided city,"[5] "city of collision,"[6] "many-bordered city,"[7] "interrupted city"[8] or "cruel city."[9] For my family and me, she remains the embracing and humane city.

While small in size, Jerusalem is large in her offerings. Walking through her alleyways, holy sites, and marketplaces, I feel the awesome energy emanating from all around me. Like other historic cities that are pluralistic—multicultural, multi-ethnic, and multilingual—she constitutes an evolving mosaic, wonderful to observe but, of even greater consequence, essential to her reshaping. The alternative is inertia, which would reduce Jerusalem to a museum piece, fit to gaze at, but never to understand. This reshaping, obviously, requires inclusion and openness, empowerment and joint action, which can turn untapped potential into realizable goals, vision into reality, and hopelessness into expectation and elated spirits.

As an evolving tapestry, Jerusalem articulates spirituality, religion, history, politics, and cultural identity. The way we connect to these expressions will ultimately either bring us closer to Jerusalem as home or distance us from her.

Jerusalem as Spiritual Place

Jerusalem is imprinted in my being and on my heart. She is the center of my existence and my destiny. Multitudes of people, my family included, experience this same reality. In Jerusalem, we are home. We sense stronger and more numerous connections than anywhere else. We feel that the Creator is in our midst, and that the Earth is nearer to the Heavens. On a clear summer night, we can touch the moon, even capture the stars!

Though Jerusalem does not have hundreds of monumental structures, she is a monument in her own right. Churches, mosques, synagogues, museums, the Old City wall (with its eight enormous exterior gates, seven of which are open), the landscapes, and the identities and interests they all represent, imbue her with sacred narratives.

Jerusalem also has an eschatological import: long-time Arab and Jewish residents; Greek and Russian pilgrims; Jewish immigrants from Europe, North Africa, and Southwest Asia; Protestant missionaries from Germany, Sweden, and the United States, among others—all have, over time, appreciated the *real* Jerusalem, but the *ideal* Jerusalem was equally important to them. They might not have seen the entire range of the tapestry but each, while rooted in a certain environment, was soaring—some preferring blue, others red or green, and still others all the shades in between. The earthly and heavenly Jerusalem, forever intertwined, still appeal to the imagination.

It is no wonder that several cemeteries surround sections of the Old City wall. Believers wish to live and be buried within the sight and sounds of the Divine, of Judgment Day. She is where I wish to rest in peace eventually as well—close to family and friends buried on the Western Hill (commonly known as Jabal Sahyoun or Mount Zion) a few feet from King David's Tomb, the Cenacle or site of The Last Supper, and Dormition Abby, where it is believed, Mary, Jesus's mother, fell into eternal sleep.

Jerusalem is not an island unto herself. She is interdependent with the region and the world. The Creator's love and our human compassion instruct that we recognize that every community and every house of worship anywhere *is* ultimately Jerusalem. Jerusalem radiates light to all, but all equally nourish her life in return. The Creator is at home where the heart is pure, where the spirit is high, and where love is embracing and unconditional.

Jerusalem as Religious Space

In varying degrees, Jerusalem expresses the actualities and visions of the Abrahamic faiths of Judaism, Christianity, and Islam. Over the millennia, she assumed importance to their "sacred geography,"[10] "… mak[ing] it very difficult for them to see the city objectively, because [she] has become bound up with their conception of themselves and the ultimate reality—sometimes called 'God' or the sacred—that gives our mundane life meaning and value."[11] (See Map 1.)

For Jews, Jerusalem is the center of their consciousness. She is, indeed, "the house of our life."[12] As a symbol of religious connectedness and national independence, her possession and safety are paramount. As such, the Israeli Jewish argument holds that returning her to Arab control, or sharing her politically with any existing or future Arab state, would endanger not only Jewish holy sites, but also Israel itself, as well as exacerbating the Israeli-Arab conflict.

For most Christians, Jerusalem is the holiest city and the center of their faith: "In Jerusalem, Christianity was born. Every Christian, every Church, was born in Jerusalem. The words of the psalm apply precisely to that spiritual but real birth and belonging: 'Everyone was born there'" (Psalm 87:5).[13] Marking the location of Jesus's crucifixion and resurrection, she is the source of inspiration for Christian meaning and salvation. Therefore, Christians hold that sharing Jerusalem and retaining a strong connection and influence there are *de rigueur* for safeguarding the Christian holy places and presence.

Interfering with the status quo that governs religious relations and space usually invites trouble. When the Jerusalem Municipality announced its intention to collect taxes from properties owned by churches in February 2018, the heads of churches in charge of the Church of the Holy Sepulchre and the status quo governing the various Christian holy sites in Jerusalem—the Greek Orthodox Patriarchate, the Custodian of

Map 1: The Old City of Jerusalem and Her Environs

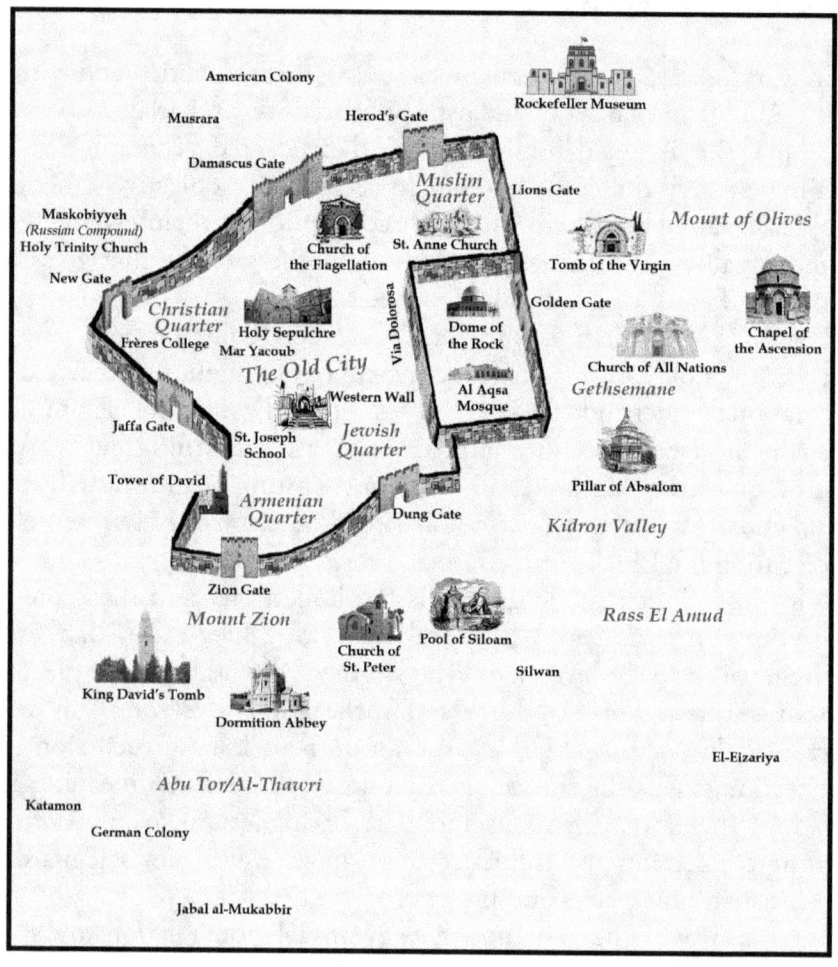

©2018 HCEF

the Holy Land, and the Armenian Patriarchate—closed the doors of the church on Sunday, February 25, protesting the municipality's "Systematic campaign against the churches and the Christian community in the Holy Land." It was not until the decision to halt tax collection that the heads of churches agreed to reopen the church on Wednesday, February 28. This unprecedented action by church leaders speaks volumes of the sensitive issues of holy sites and religious interests.[14]

For Muslims, Jerusalem is Islam's third holiest city after Mecca and Medina. She is connected with the Prophet Muhammad's Night Journey on *al-Buraq*, his celebrated steed, from Al-Masjid al-Haram in Mecca to Al-Masjid al-Aqsa in Jerusalem (Al Isra' 17:1) and his ascension to Heaven (*Mi'raj*). In addition to her religious and territorial importance, "[t]he city has strong evocative and emotional associations and has its own place in the hearts of Muslims."[15] Over the years, Jerusalem has signified communal and political independence from the occupying infidels. The Muslim argument holds that Muslim Arab control is the only way to protect Muslim sites. Israel's archaeological digs, property confiscation, and machinations since 1967 clearly indicate Israeli-Jewish designs to Judaize and control the city completely.

The sacredness of Jerusalem has amplified conflict among the three Abrahamic faiths. In a poignant account of a journey through the Middle East, William Dalrymple wrote, "In Jerusalem every street corner has its own martyr or monument, saint or shrine. Its soil is drenched in blood spilt in the name of religion."[16] This is evidenced by Jewish-Muslim tensions over the same holy compound, referred to as the Temple Mount by the Jews and Haram Al-Sharif, the Noble Sanctuary, by the Muslims. There are even intra-faith rivalries, as demonstrated by the occasional Christian disputes—among Greek Orthodox, Latin or Roman Catholic, and Armenian clergy over rights within the Church of the Holy Sepulchre—which have sometimes delayed badly needed church renovations. It is interesting to note that the custody of the door and the key for the church have been entrusted to two Muslim Palestinian families—Judeh and Nusseibeh—for over 770 years.[17] The recent renovation of Jesus's tomb, or the Holy Edicule, which began in June 2016, was completed in March 2017. The last renovation was undertaken in 1809-1810 after a major fire.

Moreover, there are aspects highlighting a tendency for Jews, Christians, and Muslims to live in the present, but exist in the past as well. This temporal dichotomy constantly compels them to plan the future to fit the past, more than to learn from or reinterpret the past to fit the present and future. While this worldview is understandable given past conflicts, fears, intolerance, and violence, it continues to divide communities, internally and externally, thus preventing compromise and reconciliation.

Jerusalem as History

Being one with Jerusalem refocuses time, compressing and elongating it to seek explanations and learn lessons. It evokes reflections from the past, both old and new. It gives fertile grounds to recollections, both pleasant and unpleasant. It considers the present and the future in the context of the land and its people, and of war and peace.

During the past 4000 years, Jerusalem's history has been partly written in blood and fire. It still stains our house of memory. Canaanites, Jebusites, Israelites, Babylonians, Assyrians, Persians, Romans, Byzantines, Arabs, Seljuks, Crusaders, Mamluks, Ottomans, and British previously walked her "holy" paths and tried to make her their home, but what remains of them are mostly archives or archeological ruins. In 1948, Jordan became the ruling power in East Jerusalem, and Israel the ruling power in West Jerusalem. Although Jordan and the Palestinians have influence in East Jerusalem, the whole city has been in Israel's hands since 1967. Over the years, Israel has extended Jerusalem's municipal boundaries to address changing realities—demographic, operational, and political—and to create irreversible facts on the ground.

Regardless of the rise and fall of tribes, empires, and nation-states, Jerusalem has recovered. Although destroyed several times, the city maintains her essence and the distinguished cultures and traditions of various peoples who call her home.

The Israeli Jewish and Palestinian Arab communities have voiced historic claims and counterclaims and erected psychological blinders that perpetuate a zero-sum game and make peace less likely. A large segment in each community has constructed distinct collective identities or has adopted partial views of history that delegitimize the history and aspirations of "the other."[18] In addition, members in each community have resorted to varying levels of violence to make their case or to retaliate, resulting in the killing and maiming of countless inhabitants, in addition to dispossession, humiliation, and impoverishment, as expressed by several wars and bloody episodes of the past.[19]

What is clear is that the language of conquerors and occupiers was, and remains, one of power and intrigue, not accommodation and reconciliation. The main goal was, and is, one of settlement, not caring, community creation, and peace building.

Jerusalem as Political Domain

Jerusalem is our collective city, but she remains challenged. As a result of winning the June 1967 War, Israel removed the barbed wire and frontier separating East Jerusalem from West Jerusalem, thus (re)unifying the city and proclaiming her its "eternal capital."

Israeli Jews and Palestinian Arabs do not view this situation in the same way. While there are interactions between them, their proximity and socioeconomic exchanges do not guarantee close friendships or warm neighborly relations. Each community uses arguments and counterarguments to discredit the other community. When reason and truth are most needed, they get buried under rhetorical layers of contrary evidence and decades of miscommunication, misinterpretation, and misunderstanding. That is not surprising given their divergent backgrounds, polarizing historical experiences, and "the lack of a consensual polity."[20]

Israeli Jews and Palestinian Arabs relate to different realities and live different lives.[21] Equally important, they "inhabit different mental worlds, informed by fundamentally different ideological axioms, infected with profound collective suspicions of each other and infused with a mutual dread that has repeatedly exploded into hate-filled aggression."[22]

It is no surprise that Israeli Jews and Palestinian Arabs do not have a meeting of minds. They compete over Jerusalem, even though the former has the upper military and political hand. Both—especially Israeli Jews—rush to buy, rent, or claim ownership of land in accordance with their differing perception of historic rights, and in anticipation of future negotiations over her status. Simultaneously, the newer sections of Jerusalem continue to expand, even while the price of land and the construction cost are astronomical, and the annual gross national product per capita—especially for Palestinian Arabs—is low. One wonders who is financing such expansion.

On December 6, 2017, U.S. President Donald J. Trump complicated matters by recognizing Jerusalem as the capital of the State of Israel. His declaration, while pleasing to most Israelis and Jews, does not only run counter to the needs and wishes of Palestinians, other Arabs, Muslims around the world, and others, but also international consensus and laws, as enshrined in United Nations resolutions, and established principles followed by prior U.S. administrations.

Jerusalem as Cultural Identity

Jerusalem is a workshop of cultural identity. She is where prophets of old and their followers walked and passed on inspiration and knowledge to others, and where the characters and personalities of multitudes were, and are, being formed. She is where we, ordinary people, want to live and let live, where we wish to raise our children with inclusive values, and where we hope to leave the world in a better condition than we found it.

Jerusalem is not discovered by attending a political lecture, listening to a guide, or reading a tourist book—although those might assist—but instead by watching people's faces. She is known by embracing the other. While there is a tendency to categorize people based on their ethnic identity and identity cards, there is much more to witness in the unique looks in their eyes and in their individual smiles or tears. These speak volumes of who they are and of their reality, aspirations, and desires. The lines in their foreheads reflect diverse backgrounds and a history more of distrust and pain than trust and pleasure, and a struggle for security, survival, and wellbeing.

Cultural identity is not static or separate from its community or web of relationships. Aspects of it do change through time, though, as they shape and are shaped by surrounding influences. Historically, the way the city's residents related to each other and to their daily existence molded them. In the latter part of the 19th century and the early part of the 20th century, Arabs and Jews lived in relative harmony. That began to change at the end of the Ottoman Empire and the First World War, when Zionism and Arab nationalism each appropriated the local identity of its own community in Palestine, creating clear distinctions and differing attitudes and behaviors toward the other.[23] These distinctions became stark as blame, conflict, and wars ravaged the land.

While the gap between Israelis and Palestinians is wide, hope for a bright future is enhanced through both a realistic appraisal of what is possible and an empathetic understanding of the other. Such new thinking and acting support learning from past lessons, responding to today's problems, and meeting tomorrow's challenges.

Jerusalem as Home

As our individual and collective home, Jerusalem requires our attention, sensitivity, and vigilance. Home is where most of our priorities and decisions are usually made: the food and drink we consume, the work we have or seek, the bills we pay, the schools our children attend, the vacations we take, the friends we keep, and the social commitments we make. Home is not all stone and mortar, though. Our aspirations and vision hold it together. Like love, we feel it when it enfolds us, when we are safe in its arms. That is why home should denote comfort, dignity, support, and trust. Home becomes even more meaningful when we share it, when we create connections within it. Enabling others to belong, especially those who less fortunate—the disabled, orphans, widows, and refugees—is a blessing.

Given Jerusalem's history of more conflict than peace, and given that most institutional religious authorities express themselves more in competition than cooperation, we must rethink our concept of *home*—the way we live and relate to others, and the way we practice our faith (not on holy days or holidays, but each day).

We must engage in the art of re-creation, in the act of re-visioning, so that we can live anew the Golden Rule. When this happens, we elevate ourselves from our individual families to our human family. We highlight common human values that promote compassion, love, hope, and peace.

We bring forth our shared—moral and practical—responsibility toward ourselves, toward each other, and toward our environment.

Jerusalem: The Home in Our Hearts

Stories are important in our own lives and in the lives of our communities. They continually form us, make us vital, and even define us. Often, they strengthen our faith, give us hope, and become gifts to future generations. In *Jerusalem: The Home in Our Hearts*, I tell my family's life story within the context of the evolution of the Holy City and the neighborhood of Al-Thawri where we lived. Drawing on an intimate knowledge of the area and of the relevant scholarly literature, I touch upon the "Jerusalem mosaic." The story contributes, albeit in a small way, to the mosaic's overall color, design, and texture. The resultant image, both multi-dimensional and nuanced, integrates and radiates facets of spirituality, religion, history, politics, and cultural identity amidst volatile conditions spanning over a century. There is no attempt to account for every event or piece of evidence, but rather to weave together those highlights—both tangible and intangible—that challenged or had meaning for my immediate family (and dear friends and neighbors).

Originally initiated to clarify what had been hidden or vague about my family's history as related to the past, to Jerusalem, and to Al-Thawri, my research evolved into a cathartic exercise that has recaptured and enlivened what is right in my own life. If my voice expresses itself now and then, it is only as an extension of my family's voice, intended to connect the story.

Arguing against dogma, double standards, extremism, and aggression, the book evolves from a familial and intellectual journey in search of balance and identity to a search for community and home. It explores what was and is in order to make sense of what is to become. That is why the book's postscript attempts to envision a more peaceful chapter in Palestinian-Israeli relations—a great wish highly valued by my family and most Palestinians and Israelis.

A defining moment in my family's story happened on June 5, 1967 at home in Al-Thawri, a historic neighborhood to the south of the Old City of Jerusalem. This date marks the eruption of the Six-Day War, which transformed not only the city's history and beyond, but also the individual lives of millions, including my family's and my own.

The narrative delves into history and relationships to trace the family's roots, distinctive backgrounds, and identities for over a century, specifically the Russian, Greek, and Palestinian origins. Of importance are the family's experiences during the 20th century and the first decade and a half of the 21st century. Among the highlights are the British Mandate, the 1948 War, Jordanian control, the June 1967 War, Israeli control, and the two Palestinian *intifadas* (uprisings against Israel) in 1978-1993 and 2000-2005, respectively.

Of special note is how women, societal networks, and common human needs impacted the lives and memories of ordinary people. First, women (my great grandmother, grandmother, mother, sisters, and others) played a central role in navigating the society's structure and the political system's paternal rules, and filling the void when male members were no longer around or able to provide adequately for their families. In so doing, they not only bore the brunt of financial and psychological stress and of inner fear, but also transformed their consciousness. They are truly "the unsung heroines."

Second, educational institutions, Western missionaries, and religious organizations provided critical services in support of learning, personal advancement, and social welfare. They acted, and still act, as safety nets in an environment often beset by aggression, oppression, unemployment, hunger, poverty, and poor health. It takes a city, it takes a community, to raise children and care for adults.

Third, while various divisions among Christians, Muslims, and Jews—and between Palestinians and Israelis—brought forth unique differences, the challenges of daily living and of the national conflict highlighted similar human concerns, ranging from the need to struggle and survive to the desire for security, peace, and a better life. Even though position and power in society have great impact, what often stands out are mutual interests and shared values that can promote cultural, national, and religious understanding.

The story ends by clarifying how transitions in Arab-Jewish and Palestinian-Israeli relations have affected my character and views, as well as those of my family members. The Afterword raises the issue of our sacred trust, mainly that Jerusalem has no room for individualistic triumphal truths, theological self-glorification, or mutual alienation of others. We—Palestinians and Israelis; Jews, Christians, and Muslims—are neighbors forever, whether we realize it and accept it or not. We must meet one another anew, as equals, and, through the process, come to an understanding of our shared mission and vision. As the poet Jalal al-Din Rumi so eloquently writes, "Out beyond all ideas // of wrongdoing and rightdoing, // there is a field. // I'll meet you there."[24]

More than the family story and the evolution of the Holy City and Al-Thawri, *Jerusalem: The Home in Our Hearts* relates to the comprehensive meaning of the pronoun "our," used to signify humanity and the right of all to partake in Jerusalem's life. Only when we allow the city to be hospitable and receptive can she fulfill her mission. In this respect, the language shies away from the national and the political rhetoric to reveal better the human dimension, even though nationalism and politics are central to the daily affairs of Jerusalem.

Jerusalem: The Home in Our Hearts also highlights the words "home" and "hearts." Home means more than a house, an airport hub, a hostel, or a temporary nest, each with its own characteristics and rules. It denotes land and space where the mind, heart, and body are in concert with each other and with the world. If home does not materialize in Jerusalem—the vibrant center of the Holy Land—where will it? If not now, when? The heart is the vital organ of life, a key to healthy living. More than the mind where reason resides, the heart appreciates and feels higher truths. It reaches out to bestow and embrace goodness and love.

Throughout the text, as has already been shown, I opt to give the city of Jerusalem feminine pronouns. While males can be nurturing, given the nature of my family's story and the support my family has received in Jerusalem over more than a century, it becomes natural to use "she" and "her" to identify Jerusalem as opposed to "he" or "it." Some words and phrases are in Arabic, French, Hebrew, Greek, Russian, and Turkish, which I have italicized and proceeded with their translation in parentheses. The book also has a few Arabic names and words with the letter ʿayn or ʿayin in them, which I have transliterated with a small c in superscript ʿ form, as in ʿAbed and *kaʿek bel semsem* (bread rings sprinkled with sesame seeds).

Jerusalem: The Home in Our Hearts would not have been written without the support of my late grandmother Futun, my late father George, my mother Evelyn, and my seven siblings: Fatina, Anastas, Khamis, Michel, Jamil, Lucy, and Elias. Their musings, stories, candor, and love over the years have made all the difference. My mother especially has been generous with her time, clarifying family and neighborly relations, explaining historic connections, and expressing her deep faith in and earnest hope for peace. It is to my family that I dedicate this book, and I alone bear full responsibility for its contents.

Heartfelt thanks are extended to my lovely wife Hiyam Zakharia Sarsar and our two gorgeous daughters NoorEvelyn and Hania for their inordinate patience and love; my sister Lucy and her children Emily, Yuhanna, and Christine for their hospitality and valuable help during my visits to Jerusalem; and George and Laila Korfiatis for sharing with me the details of the Greek side of our family tree. It is with gratitude that I also recognize Joe Ritacco for his important help in reading and providing excellent advice and editorial comments, BethSara Swanson for her superb copyediting skills, Sarah Baker for her invaluable assistance in formatting the manuscript, Hania Sarsar for designing the book cover, Christine Kattan for taking the front cover photo and Imad Zakharia for the back cover photo, and Rateb Rabie and Elias G. Saboura for their friendship and professional guidance for publishing this family memoir. Last but not least, I fully acknowledge Khader Handal's design of Map 1, depicting Jerusalem's Old City and her environs; the Palestinian Academic Society for the Study of International Affairs for Maps 2, 3, and 4; and Google for Map 5. This work was supported, in part, through a Creativity and Research Grant from Monmouth University.

Jerusalem—our city, our home—is a perfect place for checking the pulse, for hearing the heartbeat, for celebrations and songs. She calls attention to what is human, for joining conscience with hope, for realizing potential. What follows is my family's striving, starting with the June 1967 War.

Be part of the journey. See and feel the mosaic along the way.

1
War, 1967

Removed by bloody
battles, physical borders have
invaded people's brains, people's
hearts. No man's land, rich in wire—
barbed and coiled—has bred high walls—
imagined or real—dismembering lives,
crushing livelihoods. Yesterday's

shelling is history, replaced by shootings,
sharp wounds, demolitions, sirens' screams
piercing the shaky air. Saturated with more
nightmares, more traumas than dreams, adults
have passed; their children are having their own
children and grandchildren. The sun still rises
in the East. Its warm rays enliven our soul.

1967 has been described as "the year that transformed the Middle East."[25] The main reason is the Six-Day War in June 1967,[26] which was caused mainly by decades-long territorial disputes in Palestine between Arabs and Jews before 1948, followed by interstate disputes between Israel and its neighboring Arab countries after 1948.

The Arabs—the majority in Palestine for decades before 1948—wanted self-rule or independence, first from the Ottoman Empire and then from the British. Their aspirations came into competition or conflict with those of the Jews, who had longed for millennia to return from around the world to Jerusalem. While the former depended mostly on general Arab support, the latter was helped along by Zionism that emerged in the Jewish Diaspora, and by France and Britain who were victorious in the First World War. The Zionist vision of a Jewish homeland in Palestine evolved, historically, through the First Zionist Congress in Basel, Switzerland, on August 29, 1897; the Cambon Letter of June 4, 1917;[27] the Balfour Declaration of November 2, 1917;[28] and beyond.

1967 could be described more aptly as the year that transformed the individual lives of Arabs and Israeli Jews. While intelligence and military decisions were made in the weeks and days leading up to the war, the political voice was heard before and during the war. What was lacking, however, was serious consideration of how the war would impact the lives of ordinary people. One might argue that each warring side was concerned mostly about its own citizens, but neither side worried about those on the other side of the border. Perhaps this is a natural human tendency and a practical political imperative, but what we witnessed and went through as a family transformed our lives forever. It made us question authority and what we took for granted, as well as appreciate life even more so than ever before.

The Day the War Started[29]

Etched in my mind is the demarcation—or Green Line—that separated East Jerusalem (controlled by Jordan) from West Jerusalem (controlled by Israel) from 1949 to 1967.[30] Living in one of the two blockhouses on the Jordanian side adjacent to the Jordanian-Israeli frontier in Al-Thawri, my family and I saw what was known as a no man's land covered with shrubbery, prickly plants, and impenetrable rolls of barbed wire. Almost eyeball-to-eyeball, soldiers from each side of the 1948-1949 truce stood in bunkers and houses-turned-bunkers, on the lookout for the least infraction or desecration of the sanctity of their territory.

Countless sounds emanated from across this artificial border. From the hilltop, people watched from afar the panoramic view of Mount Zion, Old City, Mount of Olives, Ras al-Amud, El-Eizariya, and Abu Dis, as others sang in Hebrew or some other foreign language. Their voices ebbed and flowed with the shifting of the wind.

All this was hard for a child to understand. Those behind the fence were known as the *yahood* (Jews). Following years of animosity and distrust between Arabs and Israelis and the separation between East Jerusalem and West Jerusalem, it was not easy to know the full meaning of the border and what occurred on the other side.

Mixed with the unknown was a feeling of fear. Over the years, sniper shots killed and wounded neighbors. Border guards interrogated anyone who came close to no man's land or picked up anything thrown across the barricade. Some adults spoke of bloody happenings in *mantiqat el-haram* (the forbidden area) along the Green Line. A more fitting name would have been the Red Line! Others related horror stories of bygone days when explosions, bloody fights, and even massacres took place in Jerusalem and other cities and towns across Palestine during the British Mandate. This tenuous state of affairs was simply a continuation of the 1948 Arab-Israeli War that, in turn, was caused by decades of worsening relations between the Palestinian Arab nationalist movement and Zionism, the Jewish nationalist movement.

I was eleven years and eight months old when the war began. Like everyone else in the neighborhood, my family navigated the progression of events as best they could, acting and reacting to what was transpiring in East Jerusalem. Being one of three Christian families in an all-Muslim Arab neighborhood, we felt different at times, but remained proud of our Palestinian culture. Our home atmosphere and upbringing emphasized forgiveness, love, and peace toward the other, and that is why the war undoubtedly made us feel anxious, helpless, and uneasy, in addition to the likely dangers it contained.

The weeks preceding the war, as heard on Egyptian and Jordanian state radio stations and as exhibited by adults in Jerusalem, were filled with excitement. Many people took to the streets, overjoyed by the moves of Egypt's President, Gamal Abdel-Nasser, which included the ordering of the United Nations Emergency Force to withdraw from the Sinai on May 16,[31] the blockade of the Straits of Tiran on May 22,[32] and Jordan's King Hussein's signing of a mutual defense pact with Abdel-Nasser on May 30. Although Abdel-Nasser was loved by his own people and other Arabs, Palestinians loved him even more, as he gave them hope to reverse the *Nakba* or catastrophe that befell them during 1947-1949.[33] "All of us assumed that the humiliating debacle of 1948 was about to be avenged, and our wounded Arab pride restored.... To us, Israel was an 'entity,' a thing, at most an impersonal thorn in the flesh."[34]

For years, Hussein was trapped by both his inner tendencies and outer realities. Fighting to preserve his kingdom and survive, he was caught "between radical Nasserite Egypt and Syria, between the Arabs and the Israelis, and between his own dynastic ambitions and the passionate bitterness of the Palestinians who felt he had betrayed them."[35] It was not until Hussein reached out to Abdel-Nasser that many Palestinians began to appreciate him. His goal was "to bring Jordan back into the Arab mainstream by making a gesture of [Arab] solidarity, even though he knew that the Arabs had no hope of winning the conflict with Israel."[36] By aligning himself with Abdel-Nasser, he was putting up "a halfhearted show of resistance, as a prophylactic measure against the inevitable Arab charge that he was cooperating with the enemy."[37]

The street demonstrators shouted: "*Ashaa Hussein wa Nasser*" ("Long Live Hussein and Nasser"), "*Bil ruh bil dam nafdikuma ya Nasser wa Hussein*" ("We sacrifice our spirit and blood for you, Nasser and Hussein"), or "*Litasqut Israeel*" ("Down with Israel").

At home, no one spoke of an impending war. If a bad omen may be found early that June, it was the passing of the finch I raised for some three years. In our neighborhood, the only sign of something big about to happen was the arrival of busloads of Jordanian soldiers, mostly new recruits from the northern part of the West Bank. The recruits looked inexperienced and young, almost as young as my nineteen and seventeen-year-old brothers. They replaced some of the professional soldiers who were stationed for some time in our neighborhood. Over the years, several Jordanian officers visited with us, and I distinctly remember two of them who were friends—one was a Christian from the Bethlehem region, the other a Muslim of Bedouin stock. The military shuffle separated them, with the Christian transferred to Nablus, some 30 miles (48 km) northeast of Jerusalem, while the Muslim remained in Al-Thawri.

Although we heard some shooting over the years, no one was prepared to face the severe crisis that was about to impact us. The people's sense of invulnerability, their trust in government, and the pompous slogans and speeches of certain Arab leaders had stifled clear thinking and falsely assuaged any trepidation.

As East Jerusalemites awoke on Monday, June 5 and prepared to start another ordinary day, Radio Cairo announced the start of the fighting. Martial music, interspersed with reports, communicated high excitement and expectation. It was not until mid-morning that a few Jordanian soldiers and able-bodied men began to prepare for a possible battle by digging additional trenches and creating a connected path through the gardens and walls in the neighborhood. Property was not a concern. Some were saying, "*Bil-mal wala bil ʿyal*" ("Your possessions nothing, your families' lives everything"). To assist, women and children filled bags and pillowcases with sand and earth. The sound of small arms fire in the distance did not slow their effort.

People were even encouraged by Hussein's appeal, which was broadcast in a clear, calm voice from loudspeakers attached to the minaret:
> The time has come for us to do our duties and to achieve our aims…We are decided to live or to die honorably for those things that are most precious to all of us. Fight them (the enemy) wherever you find them…with your bare hands, with your nails, and with your teeth.

Not everyone was home. Many were still at work or on their way home. Missing from our family were my father, who was at work at the Greek Orthodox Patriarchal Printing Press and one of my older brothers, Michel, a student at Collège des Frères, who was taking a matriculation exam at Schmidt's Girls College, located opposite the Old City's Damascus Gate. We could feel the nervousness all around. "Our hands," as my mother would say, "were in hot coals."

As the war started, bus and taxi transportation stopped, and my father and brother were stuck with no way to reach home, except by foot. This meant passing close to the no man's land and being exposed to crossfire and snipers, which forced them to go the long way home: exiting the Old City from the Lions' Gate and heading toward Gethsemane, down the Kidron Valley, past Silwan (or Siloam) on their left and the Pool of Silwan on their right. They then hid in an orchard near Bir Ayyūb (Job's Well) until dusk before resuming their trek home, all the way avoiding open spaces as much as possible. Hugs and smiles welcomed their arrival.

The neighborhood turned into a ghost town as the gunfire increased and the hollow explosions of mortars joined the rattle of machine guns. Everyone was struck by the actuality of war. We were in the middle of it, and no one ever prepared us. We had no tape to stick on windows to prevent the glass from shattering if an explosion occurred. No civil defense measures were put in place. There were no air raid sirens. There were no bomb shelters. Ambulances and medical personnel were only a few miles away at al-Makassed Hospital in Ras al-ᶜAmud, or at al-Mutalaᶜ (Augusta Victoria Hospital) in At-Tur on the Mount of Olives, but it was too risky for them to reach us in a time of war. Separating us from the Jordanian-Israeli border were rolls of barbed wire, piles of sandbags, and semi-trained soldiers.

We were stranded. We had no phone. Our contact to the news—an antique electric radio—stopped as the power was cut off. Having no electricity was not too bad, since we were used to such interruptions under normal conditions and had a few kerosene lamps and plenty of candles. Anticipating a similar cut-off to our water supply, we filled every available container. In those days, we raised pigeons in the far end left corner of our garden. We made sure to keep the dovecote door open.

Only one of our two *"jiran al-hajar"* families (neighbors with whom we shared the same stone walls), headed by Abu Yahia, was home. The family members on the other side had left for their second house in ᶜAtara, a village located nine miles (15km) north of Ramallah. As neighbors, we always supported each other, and Abu Yahia, a teacher, replaced our radio as our only source of information!

After locking the front door and pulling the reception room's metal shutters closed, ten of us (paternal grandmother, father, mother, and seven children; the eighth, the oldest sister, was already married and living in Honduras) took refuge in the family's main bedroom. We assumed that its location at the center of the house—between the salon and the dining room/closed veranda—with its thick roof, walls, and doors would provide some measure of protection. Even its windows were barricaded with iron bars at least two inches thick.

We were crammed in two built-in wall closets. Our hope of survival was to stay clear of open spaces—in particular the garden, which was the target of a continuing hail of bullets coming from the east. Our movement was restricted to going to the bathroom or the kitchen. As the hours passed and the fighting worsened, we brought some kitchen utensils and food into the bedroom—or what came to be called the all-purpose room—in case sections of the house collapsed and we had to fend for ourselves for a few days.

Boom, boom, tac, tac, tac, boom. The noises still ring in my ears. To distract ourselves, we argued over whether the *boom* or *tac* was Jordanian or Israeli. We thought of our families, our friends, our neighbors. If the *boom* or *tac* were Jordanian, what was being hit on the Israeli side? How were our maternal grandfather and his family who lived in Katamon a couple of miles across the border from us? Were they hiding in their house, like us, or were they with their Jewish neighbors in a bomb shelter? How about our aunt and cousin who lived in Romema in northwest Jerusalem? And if the *boom* or *tac* were Israeli, what was being hit in Al-Thawri and the rest of the region? Were Abu Mahmoud and Imm Mahmoud, living at the no man's land and the Israeli observation point, safe? How about my friend, Awni, who lived up the street from us? How about our classmates and teachers in East Jerusalem? I tried to count all the *booms* and *tacs*, but they were so numerous and successive that the whole thing turned into a futile game. I never thought of the Jordanian shells missing their intended targets and hitting us as easily as the Israeli shells would.

An explosion here, another there. "That must have struck our next-door neighbor's house." *Boom. Boom.* Most of us were crying. "God, don't leave us now." An enormous bang hit the front door. The sound of shattering glass filled the room. With tears running down her face, my sister, Anastasia, lifted her voice in prayer, and we joined her in reciting the Lord's Prayer. (A few years later, Anastasia would become a Roman Catholic nun.) *Boom.* The walls trembled. Our room's heavily reinforced door, suitable for a vault, moved a few inches inward. The smell of gun powder permeated the air. We pushed further into the closet, hoping that layers of clothes and the closet's depth within the wall would protect us. "I am suffocating. Let me out!" *Boom. Boom.* "Be quiet; something must have hit the house." "Is everyone alright?" Intermingled with the noise of shelling and gunfire, were the sounds of sobbing, weeping, and screaming. I heard my parents asking each other: "Do you think the roof and the walls will hold any longer?" "What about cracks?" "What cracks?" As the noise subsided, I emerged into the daylight to find my father inspecting the bedroom's walls and ceiling for damage.

As the evening approached, we heard a knock on our veranda door. "It's just me. Open up." Abu Yahia came to borrow a few cigarettes, even though the grownups among us did not smoke, and to check on us. "Are you well? Is anyone hurt?" Following a short conversation, we learned that the Jordanian army had captured Government House, the headquarters of the United Nations Truce Supervisory Organization since 1948, and were proceeding to take over adjacent Israeli sites. The Israelis soon responded by capturing what was taken and pushing back the Jordanian incursion. Also, a shell had fallen on a garden in our neighborhood, killing one person, but we did not know more specifics. Given the severity of the battle, we thought it miraculous that no one else had been killed during those initial war hours.

That night, even though the exchange of fire had diminished, we remained confined to our room. The nightmarish experience of the day—the blindness of stray bullets and fear of the unknown—had immobilized us. A candle lit in front of an ancient icon glowed in the darkness and partially illuminated our sad and frightened faces. The walls reflected abstract images that contracted and expanded with the flickering of the candle. The effect was hypnotizing. When the candle finally went out and the images disappeared, almost everyone was asleep. The heavy bombardment in the distance and the exchange of fire in the neighborhood could not keep us awake. Despite the occasional snore, sleeping among friendly bodies had a reassuring and soothing quality about it.

But the feeling was only brief, for as soon as the neighborhood cocks and birds announced the coming of daybreak, the shooting intensified. Rising above the hills in the East, the sun projected its rays through the veranda windows into the house. Outside, we could hear the exchange of incomprehensible voices. As the sun rose above Jerusalem, the experience of the previous afternoon repeated—this time with the clank and clutter of machines, probably tanks, joining the ensemble of unwelcome and vexing sounds.

By afternoon, Abu Yahia came again to see us and explained that the Jordanian army had withdrawn. He advised that we leave as well. When our parents hesitated, he suggested that our father and oldest brothers should leave, as the Israelis would be harsh given the age-old hostility and tragic incidents that transpired between Arabs and Jews over the decades.

Escaping Death

Without much discussion or questioning at that time of anxiety and uncertainty, our parents took a little bag of our most precious treasures, gave a few of us small bags of food, and told us, 'Let's go." We made no argument, for we were already convinced by more than a full day of continuous bombing and shellfire. A considerable problem developed, as our grandmother refused to budge. "I am staying," she said. "If I die, let me die in my own house." All the arguments in favor of her leaving with us were for naught.

We chose to go from the garden side, as it gave us more protection than the front door side. We took a wooden ladder, went through the opening and the newly-dug trench connecting our garden to our neighbor's garden, and placed the ladder from the garden's edge down some seven feet. My father said, "Let's move quickly." My mother instructed, "Hold each other's hands and stay together." One by one, we descended, joining the exodus of neighbors and others a few yards away.

Holding hands, my eighteen-year-old brother, Michel, and I ran down the slope. Shooting was all around us. We stopped temporarily at the Al-Thawri Mosque, a familiar place to us: our neighbors prayed there and from its minaret came the *muezzin's* call to prayer five times daily. Anastasia (twenty-one years old) and Lucy (seven years old) came next, followed by my father, mother, and Jamil (sixteen years old). Khamis (nineteen years old) and Elias (four years old) had not yet arrived. ᶜAbd, one of our neighbors, was bleeding from his left hand; a bullet must have hit him. For some reason, likely a combination of fear and the fact that we did what our parents decided earlier, Michel and I resumed our flight away from the battle scene toward the East. As we ran, we saw a few women with small bundles on their heads, a frightened girl with tears in her eyes carrying a tiny baby, an old man, supported by a lad, praying as he dragged his feet along the stony path, and a couple of injured soldiers running for their lives.

It was not until sometime later that we realized we were separated from our family. We began to search, but to no avail. I wanted to return home. Michel would not permit it. The deadly sound of bombing on the horizon from whence we came prevented us from thinking correctly. Through this drama of the living and the dead, we continued running, unsure of our exact destination. Hand in hand, we jumped walls, traversed fields, and even took shelter in a chicken coop. Whatever direction we took, a shower of bullets followed. We were in the middle of the crossfire. As darkness fell, we could see the horizon behind us glowing on and off. The fighting was ongoing.

By evening, we reached another mosque, halfway between Jerusalem and Jericho, in which we spent a sleepless night among other homeless people. The cries of children, those of adults, the whispered conversations about what to do next, and the mumbling of a few older men, while telling the beads that represent the ninety-nine names of *Allah* (God)—all echoed in the huge prayer room. Except for the inconsolable crying of one or two people who must have lost a close relative or friend, silence would descend as soon as a low-flying fighter jet passed overhead or the sound of gunfire intensified in the far distance.

At dawn, as the others finished their required prayer, Michel and I resumed our flight. We decided to leave the leaderless mass and head home by an alternate route; otherwise, a few hours walk would have taken us to Ariha (Jericho). As school children, we went on fieldtrips there during wintertime, given its mild weather, either to swim in the Dead Sea or climb up the Mount of Temptation. But we were not tempted this time, as that route would take us farther from home.

Burning military vehicles, burned-out cars, and the smell of death. Nothing mattered. We wanted to find our family. Were they injured? Had they escaped like us? Would anyone be home upon our return? Memories kept surfacing, bringing us close to those people and things we missed most. We wondered if the Old City was destroyed. We repeated the same questions over and over again. We grew tired of wondering and wandering. We walked so much that our feet became partially swollen.

It was close to noon when we spotted a few houses. There was no more wilderness. What miracle was this? Where were we? At a distance, hovering in the air and floating in the midday heat, was the Greek Orthodox Monastery with the silver dome and the cross we had once visited on the way to Jericho, where my nephew was baptized in the Jordan River. The head priest, Father Theodosius, was a good acquaintance of our father, who worked for years at the Greek Orthodox Patriarchal Printing Press. We began to hurry. My feet were killing me, and my knees almost gave way beneath me. I was thirsty and hot.

A solid stone wall surrounded the monastery. The blue entrance gate appeared to be shut, but we realized that a tiny side door was slightly ajar. My brother rang the bell. A gentle-faced, middle-aged, Greek nun clad in black appeared. "Is Father Theodosios here?" my brother asked. A cool breath was coming from inside the monastery. Upon hearing the name Theodosios, the nun invited us in. Many people were sitting or standing around. A tiny church and a row of attached rooms on the right and a couple of buildings on the left became visible.

Father Theodosios, trailed by several nuns, emerged from the church and into the light of day. His black robe and black stovepipe hat contrasted wonderfully with his white beard. We hurried toward him, bowed slightly, and kissed his hand. "What sweetness?" we wondered. He and the nuns had just finished their noon prayer and must have been suffused with the sweet smell of incense. Father Theodosios insisted we stay at the monastery, at least until the war ended. Gunfire and booms were still heard in the distance. He assured us that God would neither forsake those in need of help nor ignore the pleas of those in danger.

Inside the monastery, the nuns served us *fattoush* (bread salad), lemonade, and biscuits. We offered them the bread and salty white cheese we had taken from home as we fled. We were introduced to George

Salfiti, a friend of Father Theodosios and a neighbor who lived a five-minute walk from the monastery, who knew of our family as he was friends with Nasser Mukhar and his sister, Mary Mukhar, our godparents who lived in Amman, Jordan.

In late afternoon, we were shown to one of the tiny rooms adjacent to the church. As befitting the residence of a monk and ascetic nuns, the room was rather plain, with two single beds, a chair, a small table, and a cross hanging on the wall. There were two tiny windows, a square one overlooking the Jerusalem-Jericho road and a round one above the door that opened on to the monastery's courtyard. Exhausted and anxious, but no longer hungry or hot, we retired to our room. I went to sleep. I do not even remember saying my prayers.

At dawn, there was much activity at the monastery. Additional people came into the courtyard. One was shot in the head, with the bullet grazing his right ear and the side of his face. George, who knew first aid, placed a bandage on his wounds and advised him to seek medical care, whenever it became safe to travel to Makassed Hospital or Augusta Victoria Hospital.

We also learned that Father Theodosios and the nuns had been asked to look after the abandoned animals at an adjacent Siniora Farm, whose owners fled to Amman. As my need to be useful was great, and the groaning of the cows was unbearable, I offered to be put to work. In Al-Thawri, we raised chickens, pigeons, and birds, but since I had never had the opportunity to milk cows, one of the nuns provided me with a crash course.

That afternoon, our movement outside the monastery was restricted by an Israeli-imposed curfew. Father Theodosios and the nuns sought sanctuary in the church. They prayed and chanted, and we joined them. Votive lamps with colorful Christmas balls hung from the decorated ceiling. Icons blessed the walls. In one, Jesus raised Lazarus from the dead, as his sisters, Mary and Martha, watched. Another depicted Jesus's triumphal entry into Jerusalem. The Virgin Mary and baby Jesus looked on from above a side altar. The candlelight illuminating the darkness, the liturgical melodies, and the scent of incense had cathartic and hypnotizing effects.

While concerned about the war and its impact on the lives of innocent people, Father Theodosios spoke of his full trust in God and counseled us to do the same. He was ready for the hereafter and had built himself a tomb, adorned with flowers and plants, just outside the church.

Our stay ended on the third day when George and his wife, Rahmeh, invited us to spend some time with them. They were kind and did their best for us, providing us with room, board, and even a bucket bath, as water was scarce. Aside from errands to the monastery or to buy bread (baked on hot slabs) at a nearby Bedouin encampment, we remained in the house. The prevailing impression was that it was dangerous to come face-to-face with Israeli soldiers.

A tragedy almost happened when Michel, not aware of the curfew hours, walked a few doors down the road to deliver bread to two elderly sisters, friends of the Salfiti family. An over-zealous Israeli soldier put a gun to his head, vowing to execute him. An officer jumped in the middle and calmed matters. "Don't you see? I am trying to deliver bread to two old ladies!" Michel addressed the soldier defiantly. "No, I wasn't afraid," Michel remembered. "I don't know why."

The days I spent at the home of the Salfiti family were among the longest of my life. From dawn to darkness, my fears were exacerbated by the fears of those around me. Another person can comfort someone with a private sorrow, but when everyone is frightened, there is no place to turn. My mind kept bringing back thoughts of my family in Al-Thawri and of Jerusalem. I couldn't think of one without the other.

On the third day with the Salfitis, we heard that the war had ended and that people were resuming their "normal" life. My brother went scouting a route to ensure that our journey home would be safe. With much anticipation, I waited through the long afternoon. Lying on a sofa on the balcony overlooking the hills, I was carried away by apprehension and concern. I fell asleep. It seemed I was standing at our garden's edge in Al-Thawri, looking out at the vista encircling the Old City. Suddenly, the sky darkened, the clouds thickened, and torrents of rain gushed down to the earth. I had never witnessed so much water in my life. Miraculously, I remained dry. I tried to move, but my feet extended downward, penetrating the soil until they touched the deepest rocks. No one was there to help. The rain kept falling and the water level kept rising, submerging everything in its way. The city stood surrounded by water. In the distance, a flock of tiny sparrows appeared. As they ascended, the clouds began to part and quickly disappeared, ending in a flash of bright light at the gate of the seventh heaven. I awoke!

My brother returned the next day. He relayed that the way home was accessible and described how, upon approaching Bir Ayyūb (Job's Well), he found our family members, who were just returning from hiding in Beit Sahour, a town adjacent to Bethlehem. Happy ululation and cries filled the air.

Ecstatic with the good news, we bade farewell to the Salfitis and resumed our trek. As we moved along, structures on the horizon became familiar again. With a powerful instinct to guide us, we headed home. Time passed quickly, and soon we could see the edge of our garden and the contour of our home. We found that the ladder we used while escaping was still there. I saw no angels coming down to help, so I climbed up to the welcoming hands of those most close.

Our Family's Ordeal

The war presented both us and our neighbors with a reality that we were never prepared to handle. Some became compulsive talkers, reenacting everything they experienced. Others remained introspective or in shock. The inner world became easier to penetrate than before the war.

Obviously, I wanted to share the experience Michel and I went through with our family and anyone else who would listen. I was just as eager to hear our family's story and how we separated from each other on the afternoon of Tuesday, June 6. Michel and I told them of the hospitality shown to us by Father Theodosios and the Salifti family. Our father actually knew Father Theodosios. He often met him as he brought typesetting requests to the Greek Orthodox Patriarchal Printing Press. He spoke glowingly of him, saying: "His care and kindness are boundless."[38]

As for our family's side of the events, we learned that during our flight, our mother realized in the Al-Thawri Mosque that Khamis and Elias were missing. Leaving the rest of the family there, she returned to search for them. The hissing sound of bullets zooming past her, shouts in Arabic instructing her to get down into the trench, and the recurring thoughts of worse things to come did not halt her advance. "Have you seen my two sons?" she repeatedly asked. As she continued, a voice ordered her to stop. It was not a Jordanian soldier, as she assumed, but an Israeli officer, as she would come to find out. "I am looking for my sons, two of them. Have you seen them?" she asked with a quivering voice. A moment of dreaded silence followed. With tears in her eyes, my mother told him their ages, describing their features and hoping the officer, despite his machine gun, would respond with sympathy. He spoke in broken Arabic.

The officer was neither Jordanian nor Iraqi, as some neighbors initially thought; yet there was a rumor that Iraqi soldiers had reached the area to reinforce the Jordanian army. A neighbor even applauded upon seeing an "Iraqi" military unit, only to receive a bullet in the palm of his left hand. Iraqi soldiers were addressing people in broken Arabic and each other in Hebrew!

While people fled, Israeli soldiers had occupied the area and detained everyone they found in their way. Khamis, with Elias in his arms, was the last one to come down the ladder. He missed the last rung, falling down; as he rose up, a redheaded soldier in full battle gear directed him to the house across the way, that of Abu Sliman. "It's a miracle that no bullets hit us," Khamis recalled, "neither from the Jordanians nor from the Israelis."

My mother was also directed to the same house. Inside were frightened people, some huddled together, others kneeling or lying down, hoping to escape the bullets being fired from a distant hill. Standing guard while simultaneously responding to fire from the opposing Jordanian army were Israeli soldiers.

In a far corner of the house, my mother spotted two familiar faces. With tears running down her face, she jubilantly cried, "Here you are. Thank God." Bending down below a windowsill and holding Elias as if to form a shield was Khamis. "These are my sons. Can I take them now?" my mother asked the nervous officer in a hurried voice. "My oldest is only a student; he studies at Collège des Frères; he knows nothing about what is happening." "Wait," the officer replied. "My son is only a student; please release him," she pleaded. Luckily, Khamis had his school identification card with him. After the soldier inspected it, he was set free. Disregarding the shooting and overcoming her fear, albeit temporarily, my mother continued her plea: "Let me fetch the rest of my family. They are at the mosque. Allow us to return home. We don't want to harm anybody. We want to live in peace."

A while later, my mother, my father, and our siblings were allowed to return home. The soldier asked them to hang a white cloth from the main door. As they started to climb up the ladder, they were horrified to see the body of a dead man on the ground a few yards away. Upon closer inspection, it was Abu Yusuf, our neighbor. When my grandmother saw them come back so soon, her surprise turned to terror when she found out that Michel and I were missing. My father and Anastasia reassured her, saying, "We saw them. They left with the others who were at the mosque, but we do not know in what direction they headed." They spent a sleepless night, worrying about us and what was going to happen next and praying the Holy Rosary. The battle for the Old City and the rest of East Jerusalem continued.

It was not long after dawn the next day that Israeli soldiers knocked on our front door. In broken Arabic, they ordered all to leave: "*inzel takht ʿind ihssain*" ("Go down to Hussein"), probably meaning that our family should leave for Jordan. My mother pleaded with them, explaining that her father lived in West Jerusalem, and rather than becoming homeless in Jordan, she wanted to go to him in Katamon. The soldiers, fully armed, were in no mood to entertain any such idea.

With no choice, my family, including my grandmother this time, took some food, locked the doors, and went down the wooden ladder. Our grandmother had the hardest time. Her heart was set against leaving, and the spaces between the ladder rungs were wider than she expected, and the distance from top to bottom of the ladder was long. Instead of going toward the East, as we did the day before, they headed southward. My youngest sister, Lucy, carrying two medium-size baskets containing home-baked bread and pressed white cheese, used the baskets to push the prickly plants and shrubs out of our grandmother's way. The pace was slow, as our grandmother had weak knees. By late afternoon, they reached a large, clean cave—probably a Bedouin dwelling—where more than a few people were resting for the night.

At sunrise, Anastasia and Jamil went ahead of everyone else to explore the road to Beit Sahour, the town east of Bethlehem. After passing to the east of Jabal Abu-Ghneim, houses began to show on the horizon. Anastasia asked the first person they met about the location of the home of Mikhaeel Abu Sᶜdah, her high school teacher (and after the war, mine and my younger sister's teacher as well), and his family. Mr. Banourah showed them the way and even invited them to stay at his own house.

Like George and Rahmeh Salfitis, Mikhaeel and Afifeh Abu Sᶜdah were hospitable and kind. My family was given a room and all the necessary amenities. The Abu Sᶜdah children played with my siblings. Neighbors popped in and out to inquire about the status of the war and to show their compassion. Much time was spent in the garden, appreciating the June sun, even though the air was tense all around. When not listening to the news on radio, the adults talked about what had transpired and how life under Jordan might change under Israel. Mikhaeel, an active member of the Beit Sahour town council, had his pulse on the daily happenings. Although it was premature to reach any conclusions, there was agreement on what appears first to be a simple fact: "Life is precious, but unpredictable." While we must be ready for its twists and turns, they concurred, "ultimately, we are all in God's hands." Though perhaps more philosophical and deterministic than expected, it was befitting another tragic moment in our life and history.

A couple days after the war ended, my family extended heartfelt thanks to the Abu Sᶜdah family and headed northward toward home—the destination clear, but the journey difficult. Even though they stopped frequently, the lack of a bathroom facility and the hot June sun proved challenging. Our grandmother had a hard time walking. There came a point when she sat down to rest and refused to get up, saying: "Leave me and go on. I will manage on my own. Leave me to the wild beasts!"

Our father went searching for an alternative mode of transportation. He eventually found a Bedouin who was willing, for a small fee, to rent his donkey, which made the way a bit easier. Imagine my grandmother riding a donkey through *alttalal wa alwidyan* (the hills and valleys) of the desert!

The Battle in Abu Tor/Al-Thawri

Our ordeal as a family was serious. Thankfully, we all made it out alive. Other neighbors were adversely affected, but so were the residents on the other side of no man's land, as well as those of other neighborhoods on both sides of the border in Jerusalem and the larger region. The battle in Abu Tor/Al-Thawri was not as devastating as in other areas, but it was deadly nevertheless.

The initial shelling we heard mid-morning on June 5 had come from the Jordanian side, probably from Ras al-Amud, Abu Dis, and El-Izzariya on the east of us, taking aim at targets to the West of us. As we hid that early afternoon, major firing intensified just across the valley from Al-Thawri, and that is when Jordan's 31st Battalion, commanded by Col. Badi Awad, captured the UN headquarters, located in Jabal al-Mukabbir, forcing UN employees, including some of their family members, to take shelter in one room. They survived an ensuing twenty-five-minute battle between Jordanian and Israeli soldiers, which involved two Israeli fighter jets assisting and resulted eventually in the Israeli takeover of the UN headquarters. What followed was another bloody fight extending from the UN headquarters outward toward Sur Baher to the south of Al-Thawri.

The actual battle in Abu Tor/Al-Thawri did not begin until around 2:30 Tuesday afternoon. There was an Israeli post opposite each Jordanian post. A source presenting the Israeli version of events details that "From south to north there were, on the Jordanian side, [what the Israeli army called] the 'Lulav Post,' the 'Crown House Post,' the 'Lion Post,' the 'Platoon House,' and the 'Yellow Shutters House.'"[39]

Obviously, we did not know the names of these posts, but all were near our house, which was situated in the second row of blockhouses. We did not know who the Jordanian soldiers were, or how many of them were there to secure our neighborhood. Similarly, we knew nothing about those fighting on the Israeli side.

The Jerusalem Brigade, an Israeli reserve unit led by Colonel Michael Peikes, was put in charge of the operation. Four companies, A-D, were mobilized, with A targeting the "Lulav Post" and then the "Crown House Post," B targeting the "Lion Post," C targeting the "Platoon House," and

D the "Yellow Shutter House." As these posts were cleared, the three platoons would then proceed, as instructed by Captain Eli: "The first platoon would take the front-line blockhouses. The second would dash halfway down the hill and block the road, which divided the village laterally. The third platoon would then move through to mop up the area between the blockhouses and the road."[40]

By all accounts, the battle was fierce. The Jordanian military shelled Israeli positions from the stone houses. The shelling was accurate and severe. There was definite coordination between the Jordanian military stationed in Al-Thawri and those stationed across the Hinnom Valley on Mount Zion. The Israeli soldiers responded in kind.

As we were crying, praying, and preparing to leave "our shelter" for a safer location, Jordanian and Israeli soldiers were killing each other. Israeli tanks at the UN headquarters in the south fired ahead of the troops to clear their path in Abu Tor/Al-Thawri: explosions…a mortar barrage…a smoke screen down the hillside…a Jordanian sniper taking out Israeli soldiers…an Israeli soldier neutralizing him with a grenade…tanks…three barbed wire fences…brush and thorns…heavy machine gun fire…hand-to-hand combat…much blood…lifeless bodies. Jordanian soldiers who were able to escape ran down the slope and disappeared into the mass of people fleeing the battleground.

When the battle in Abu Tor/Al-Thawri ended, the neighborhood "was choked with hazy, sweet, pungent smoke rising from charred wood, rubber, uniforms, hair and muscle."[41] Zakaria el-Bazlamit "saw the bodies of bloodied, broken Jordanian soldiers behind garden walls. The hillside was peppered with bullet casings and shrapnel."[42] The Israeli toll was equally high. As the Jerusalem Brigade commander inspected the area when the shooting was over, he saw "a dead soldier being borne up the slope on a stretcher. As it passed, [Colonel Eliezer] Amitai looked down at the lifeless face of Michael Peikas."[43]

The immediate outcome in Abu Tor/Al-Thawri: Israel won the battle and took over Al-Thawri, but at what cost? Seventeen dead and sixty-five wounded. Jordan lost the battle and Al-Thawri, but at what cost? Many dead and wounded soldiers, but we never heard the number. Abandoned barracks were riddled with bullets. A couple of them had fire scars. They stood bare and empty—not as memorials for those who died, but because their owners were not around to reoccupy them.

No one from either Jordan or Israel has ever apologized to us. It seems that the survivors—the traumatized—must manage somehow. And the dead must be remembered.

A memorial, a marble plaque, in the public park off Ein Rogel Street[44] in Abu Tor commemorates the Israeli dead. There is no monument in Al-Thawri dedicated to the common memories of Jordanian soldiers and civilians killed during the war. Perhaps prayers were recited on their behalf. Vanquished soldiers receive no medals.

While there were victors and vanquished, a memorial for all the dead and for all the survivors—or rather for peace—is most fitting. Such a memorial would be best if it were jointly designed by Palestinians and Israelis. Its perfect location would on the old border that once separated East Jerusalem from West Jerusalem.

Humanizing the enemy creates possibilities, as it softens hearts and minds. Meron Benvenisti, an Israeli historian and former Deputy Mayor of Jerusalem, stated, "When people die, no political accounts remain, and the memory of the dead should be honored."[45] I say: When people live, the memory of the dead lives through them, and the memories of the survivors make certain that mistakes of the past are not relived.

Our Traumatized Neighborhood

Inspection of our immediate surroundings pointed to explosive shells that landed on the two neighbors' houses on either side of us. One mortar shell got lodged in the thick domed roof of our family's main bedroom, where we had hidden during the battle. Another mortar shell, bent, rested on the ground right outside our front door. It was less than ten feet from our hiding place. Imagine if both had exploded. A bomb squad came a few days later and collected the two shells.

Stories of suffering and death spread throughout the neighborhood. Awni, with whom I had played as a child, spent time watching the battle from the garden's edge. He was hit by a shell and killed instantly. Some said, "He was buried where he fell, in the garden." Abu Yusuf, a quiet and nonviolent man, was another victim. The two Jordanian officers who used to visit us were killed—one as he fought from the bunker facing Mount Zion, and the other in Nablus.

Some neighbors related how the Israeli soldiers had terribly scared those who stayed behind. Adult men were forced out of their houses and made to walk with their hands up to the Israeli command station where they were interrogated. Others spoke of how their houses were looted by neighbors from the other side who were armed with guns and metal bars.

Abu Ghazi, our next-door neighbor who took his family to be safe in ʿAtara, died of a broken heart. His hero was Gamal Abdel-Nasser. The Arab defeat and Abdel-Nasser's decision to resign[46] were both devastating and a personal defeat for him. His house in Al-Thawri was ransacked. His bedroom's large cupboard had bayonet scars. The large photo of Abdel-Nasser above his king bed was broken—the imprint of a soldier's combat boot marking its shattered center. Glass fragments were strewn over the pillows and bedcover.

Abu Yahia and his family fled but never returned. That was the fate of other neighbors. It is possible that they crossed to the East Bank of the Jordan River. Some of these Palestinians ended up dying or suffering terribly, along with Jordanians, during Black September, the Civil War between September 1970 and July 1971. It is equally possible that Abu Yahia and his family were repatriated to the West Bank with other Palestinians in the months and years past the war. No one knows for sure what happened to them.

Through the trauma of the living and the dead, we experienced déjà vu soon after we returned home. The war was still extremely fresh on our minds. With a curfew in place and for an unexplained reason, the Israeli military conducted some reenactments of the battle in Abu Tor/Al-Thawri. We heard a few hollow explosions. From behind the glass of closed windows, we saw soldiers, battle ready and fully armed, rushing down the hill opposite our house and bearing to the right of the street past the reddish house and the fig tree. The Israeli military also set up a watch tower atop the roof of a neighbor's two-story house, five doors to the north of our house. Even though it might have been for security purposes during those dangerous times, most neighbors viewed it as an act of intimidation.

To our great surprise, there was a knock at our front door that week and, low and behold, our maternal grandfather, Jani, was waiting impatiently to see us. We had mutually worried: we about him and his family, and he about us. The access points between East Jerusalem and West Jerusalem were not yet open, at least for those in East Jerusalem. The dangers of no man's land and military restrictions did not impede his way from Katamon in West Jerusalem: "I am David Ben Gurion![47] I am here to see my daughter and her family." Laughing out loud, he repeated what he told the Israeli soldiers at the military checkpoint. His main concern was to ensure that we were safe and had sufficient provisions. Upon leaving, he made certain to speak with the Israeli soldiers on our street, saying among other things: "*shalom*" ("salaam" or peace), "*kulanu bnei adam*" ("We are all human"), and "*zeh mishpacha sheli*" ("That's my family"). While we could only recognize a couple of Hebrew words at that time, what he was actually asking them to do was to take good care of us and, by inference, everyone else in our neighborhood.

As we waited for more changes to come, we filled the trench running through our garden that was dug the day the war started. We fixed the holes in the garden walls between us and our neighbors. We, especially my father, listened intently to several radio broadcasts, including the BBC and those from Jordan, Egypt, and Israel. We read the local newspapers, knowing well that a new city order, a new era, was taking shape....

2
POST-WAR ECHOES

War sounds dissipated.
Authority, once magical,
lost its luster. Drumbeats
of the day after war,
power-driven, confused
the heart, the mind too.
What either of them felt,

the other did not believe.
People got older fast,
maturing quicker than usual!
Much soul searching
discovered diverse tunes
as drummers marched to their own
rhythms of no war, no peace.

The June War lasted only six days but it enabled Israel to quadruple its size by seizing East Jerusalem and the West Bank from Jordan, the Gaza Strip and the Sinai Peninsula from Egypt, and the Golan Heights from Syria (Map 2). The declarations, practices, and reverberations that followed the war continued to be felt in every heart and at every corner. These had the sobering effect of giving birth to new realities.

Questions were abundant; answers were few. Sometimes it took a long time to understand their meanings and implications. The war was described as "miraculous." Was its outcome—Israeli victory and Arab defeat—engineered by God or by humans? What have the ordinary people—on the vanquished or victorious side—done to deserve it? How will Israel, filled with euphoria and prowess, treat the conquered Palestinians, filled with anxiety and resentment? What will tomorrow bring?

A Transformative Time

People's sheltered lives in Al-Thawri and the rest of East Jerusalem came to a temporary halt. What was previously taken for granted became challenged. Authority turned into a skeleton, devoid of legitimacy and propriety. Those unhappy with the *fait accompli* began to pay more attention for ways to survive the forced change that was underway. They also started to think of a new cadre of Palestinian leaders who promised liberation of Palestine, as was enshrined in the Palestinian National Charter of 1964 and 1968, respectively (until it was modified following the signing of the Oslo Accords in September 1993).

Each generation responds to change in its own way. My parents managed the British Mandate and Jordanian rule, just as their parents had to deal with Ottoman rule and the British Mandate. In the months and years following June 1967, we had to come to terms with the aftereffects of the war and the new reality of a unified Jerusalem. There was no choice but to face the change head on.

There was hesitancy at the start, a feeling not to trust. The changes challenged everyone's attitudes, activities, and surroundings. We debated the nature and extent to which such changes would influence our security, commitments, and lifestyles. Our lives and livelihoods—work, schools,

Map 2: Territories Occupied by Israel in June 1967

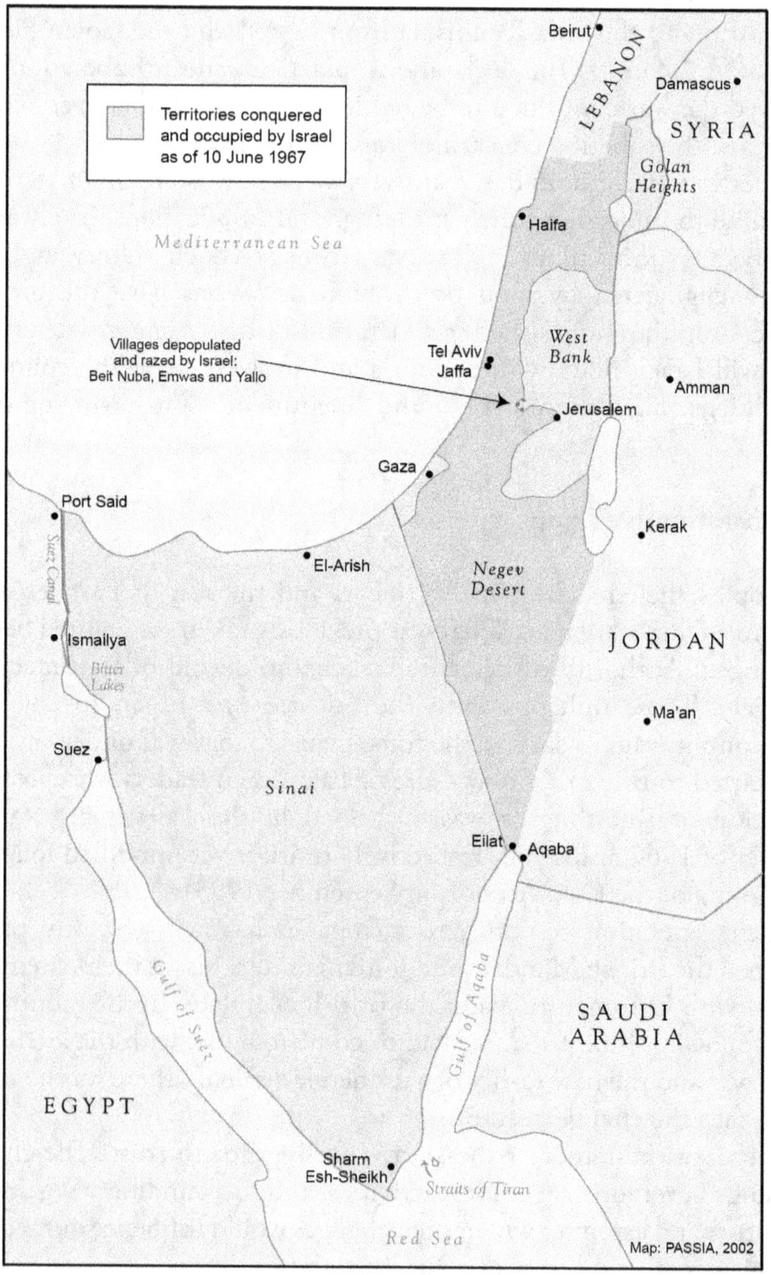

churches, markets, relatives, and friends—were still in East Jerusalem, but the center of government and power was in West Jerusalem. Whenever we were confused or uncertain about our new conditions, we took solace in the fact that familiar realities awaited us home in Al-Thawri.

Even though relationships between Arabs and Jews were renewed or newly formed, life in general—and in Jerusalem in particular—was experienced differently by, and within, each national community. Some drew closer to God: the Arabs among them, both Christians and Muslims, gave thanks to Allah for not totally forgetting them, and hence became more observant or straightened their path; the Jews among them gave thanks to the *Elohim* (the Hebrew name for the same God) for watching over them and giving them victory, and hence became less secular. Tough times make people grow closer to God and to each other. For others, whether concerned or relieved, the barbed wire and prickly plants continued to reside in their brains. They remained stagnant in old attitudes and behaviors, believing their own side's narrative, not the other side's story. Still others became depressed, frustrated, and humiliated by the whole experience. Dr. Amin Majaj—our pediatrician for years, former titular mayor of Jerusalem, and former Jordanian Minister of Health—had "confined himself to his home," and it took several months until he resumed his regular schedule.[48] In contrast, there were those who saw benefit in change and compromise, but without necessarily sacrificing their community ideals and individual aspirations. By thinking of the past, they refused to be imprisoned by it. Instead, the present became their path toward actualizing potential.

The Israeli presence brought about major changes. In the midst of permanence, these changes modified our conceptions of time and space. Post-war realities began to replace old ones, while traditional, communal, religious, and national tendencies attempted to enliven and strengthen the past. Some of our friends were even asserting the transience of the present and a wish for the return of Arab rule.

Despite such concerns, Israeli actions and decisions made their way in our city. We considered Israel's policy declarations and international positions. As soon as it became permissible, we crossed the border into "the enemy's forbidden world." We acclimated to the new reality as we absorbed the winds of change going through our lives—economically, legally, and otherwise. We, the pupils, returned to school.

The days following the war witnessed, among other things: house-to-house searches for Jordanian soldiers and weapons, arrests and interrogation of Palestinian civilians, instances of maltreatment, looting by Israeli civilians and soldiers, the removal of the bodies of dead soldiers, the burial of dead civilians, and the clearing of no man's land.[49]

The Israeli government, asserting its military force and political influence, began re-configuring the Old City, which it annexed in 1967, and the rest of East Jerusalem, which it annexed thirteen years later. There was news of the destruction of Harat al-Magharibah (the Moroccan Quarter) across from the Western Wall, which housed around one hundred families, or 650 people. While "the presence of the Holy" was a factor,[50] there was also a practical consideration—mainly the need to accommodate hundreds of thousands of worshippers per day, instead of a few thousand as had occurred during the British Mandate.[51]

The Israeli government also enacted laws regarding Jerusalem's sovereignty, municipal government, and Holy Places, after passing related bills through the *Knesset* (Israeli parliament) during the last few days of June 1967. These extended the jurisdiction of the Israeli West Jerusalem Municipality to East Jerusalem, dissolved by military order the Arab East Jerusalem Municipality—along with the dismissal of the Arab mayor and his council—and provided safeguards to the Holy Places (Map 3).[52]

Even though a child at the time, I heard about the ongoing changes and the general parameters of official declarations. My parents, grandmother, and others were hearing about and discussing them, as these changes had direct implications on our daily lives.

Most Palestinians of East Jerusalem, and others around the world, did not receive these and other changes well. They viewed them as counter to United Nations resolutions and illegal under international law.[53] My family preferred an international status for Jerusalem, given its spiritual and multi-religious appeal and the minority position in which the Living Stones or Holy Land Christians found and still find themselves, irrespective of the sovereign power in control. Over the years, the League of Nations viewed Jerusalem as "a sacred trust of civilization," that must be protected; the UN favored a special status, with separate

Map 3: Pre- and Post-1967 Jerusalem's Municipal Boundaries

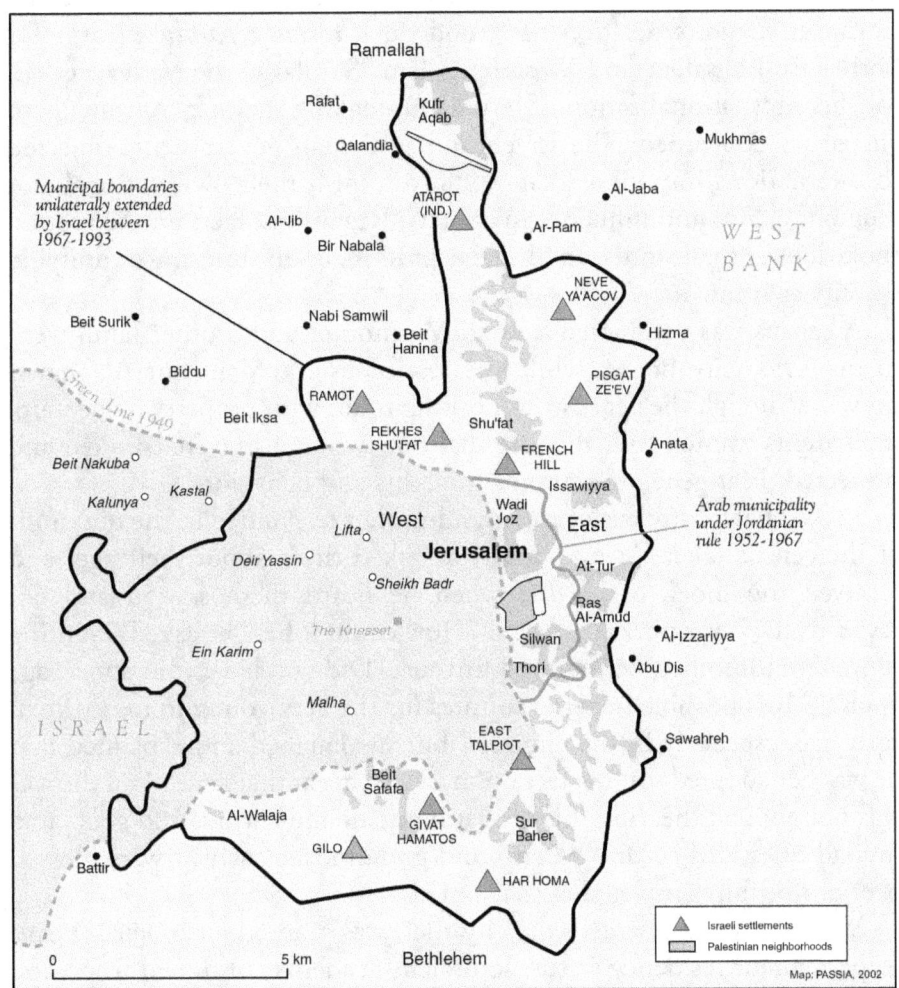

legal and political arrangements for East Jerusalem, as enshrined in UN General Assembly resolution 181 (II) of November 29, 1947; and the European Union's position has stood for a *corpus separatum* status for both East Jerusalem and West Jerusalem. Similarly, the Vatican called for the internationalization of Jerusalem, making the case continually to all parties concerned. The Israeli and Jordanian governments objected to internationalization, as that would diminish their own national and religious claims and influence in the city. Regardless, facts on the ground spoke louder than words, and Israel kept its focus on annexing or unifying the city as it saw fit.

A census was conducted as well. My mother and brother Jamil went to our Old City house, while the rest of us stayed in our Al-Thawri house. Although the census had nothing to do with property ownership, my parents wanted to make sure that our two houses were counted and protected. Fear generated strange thoughts and behaviors.

In Al-Thawri, my father and grandmother responded to the questions of the census taker. At one point, he asked them about their ages and received the shock of his life when he heard them say 54 and 66, respectively. I was puzzled as well. "How could it be?" he asked. Pointing to my grandmother, he inquired further: "Did you have your son at age twelve?" It is possible in some cultures for the very young to marry at an early age, especially in the old days, but she laughed and explained that he was her adopted son—a fact unknown to me at that time. As if the war was not enough, hearing this revelation made me curious and generated myriad questions for my parents and grandmother, which were glossed over or not fully answered at that time.

Whoever was present in the city then was granted an Israeli ID card or permanent residency status. Jerusalem residents continued to possess Jordanian citizenship given to them starting in 1954. This ID card enabled traveling within Jerusalem, the newly conquered Palestinian territories, and Israel. Those living in the West Bank and the Gaza Strip had a more difficult time traveling in and out of their locales. All of us, however, had to submit to questioning if stopped by police or military patrols, or when exiting and reentering Israel or Israeli-controlled areas. In addition, being a resident of Jerusalem obligates one to pay taxes, but also qualifies one to have the right to vote in municipal elections, participate in the administrative affairs of the city, and receive social security benefits and state health care.

Crossing the Now Invisible Border

With the removal of the barbed-wire fences and the clearing away of mines and other obstacles in the no man's land, there was nothing keeping us from crossing the border. The Green Line, drawn on a map in November 1948, had no visible markings on the ground or in the air! There was excitement, but it was tinged with anxiety. There was curiosity, but as young people, our interest was to discover where our grandfather, Jani, and his family lived; for our parents, it was a journey of rediscovery. The unknown was yet to become familiar; for our parents, the known was yet to become more familiar. In either case, the journey was our initial attempt to overcome trauma and achieve normalcy in an otherwise abnormal environment.

My brothers, Khamis and Jamil, preceded us. If they did not wish to walk the entire way, our mother advised them to take Bus #4 and ask the driver where to get off for Hashayarot Street. That was the same bus number she used before the division of Jerusalem in 1948.

As for us, we rushed to ascend the dirt incline toward the observation spot from where the pre-June 1967 sounds emanated. Shrubs and barbed wire were still visible on the hill to our left. Our mother pointed to Mount Zion and the burnt-out dome of the Church of the Dormition, as our father led the way on the road (Ein Rogel Street) he used to walk many times prior to 1948, when he worked at the [British] Government Printing Press across the street. The Windmill, the King David Hotel, and the YMCA tower appeared on our right horizon. Nearer to us, towering on the nearest hill, we saw St. Andrew's Scots Memorial Church, built in remembrance of the Scottish soldiers who died fighting the Ottoman army during the First World War.

Upon reaching the first intersection at Hebron Road, the whitish building of what used to be the Government Printing Press came into full view, as throngs of jubilant people headed in the direction of the Old City, a short walk away. Unlike the negligible traffic of Al-Thawri, Abu Tor had a constant flow of modern buses and cars. Next, on the left, was the railway station (the first I have seen in my life) with its tracks initiating the path to the Mediterranean coast; a low wall and a barred-metal fence on top of it directed us around the bend to what we would later come to know as Emek Refa'im Street. Our father remembered the gas station on the right and the German Colony a little further down on the left. Soon enough, opposite a Protestant cemetery, we turned right and walked past Arab houses, built with Jerusalem stone, with arched windows and balconies. These were interspersed between more industrial-looking Israeli apartments and houses. Mature cypress and pine trees—most likely planted by Arab owners in the 1930s and 1940s before they went into exile—mixed with newer climbing plants. Our mother spoke of how the open spaces of the 1940s had disappeared: "On my way to visit my father," she told us, "I used to stop with my friend, Katie Nuzha, to play in the fields where these two houses stand, and we would pick red *hanoon* (anemone coronaria) and *qarn el-ghazalle* (cyclamen)." Our walk eventually took us to 10 Hashayarot Street, where our grandfather received us with open arms.

Like tourists returning from a brief visit to a foreign land, we instantly became "experts" on almost everything we observed. Our grandfather and his family became our bridge to the unknown and untried. They even put us on exhibition whenever we visited them by introducing us to their friends and neighbors, who, in turn, bombarded us with questions about our recent, and not so recent, past: "How did it feel living on the other side? Were you treated properly? What have you seen thus far?" Everyone was exploring everyone else's world.

Some twenty years later, Hala Sakakini described in her book, *Jerusalem and I*, a similar visit that she and her sister, Dumia, paid to their house after nineteen years in exile. The Sakakinis—along with other Palestinian families, as well as Greeks, Armenians, and Russians—lived in the same neighborhood as our grandfather. For Hala and Dumia, their visit was unpleasant, and for understandable reasons: Katamon was denuded of its Palestinian inhabitants, the neighborhood was no longer familiar, and the Sakakini house was taken over by Israelis and turned into a nursery and kindergarten.[54]

Adjusting to a New Reality

The older generation who had gone through the Arab Revolt of 1936-39 and/or the 1948 War had a larger context for what was happening. The youth did not. They were catapulted from boyhood to adulthood. There was no time for adolescence, as life was transformed overnight, and its challenges had to be faced regardless of age, ideology, national inclinations, religious belief, or socioeconomic standing.

The border's opening gave easy access to the Old City and beyond. There was no longer the need to travel from Al-Thawri through the Silwan, Kidron Valley, and Gethsemane areas, as was done during Jordanian times. We simply headed west on Ein Rogel Street, turned right on Hebron Road for a two-minute ride or a ten-minute walk to the Old City. We would pass the Valley of Hinnon on our right and Mishkenot Sha'ananim, the windmill, the King David Hotel, and the Sultan Pool on our left, before entering through the only non-walled section of the Old City, a few feet or so from Jaffa Gate. Sometimes, we opted to go the old route if we were closer to it than to Jaffa Gate, or if we just wanted to re-experience one of our past routes.

Amid the "normalcy," business in and outside the Old City witnessed a boom, as Israelis took advantage of the variety of goods and the lower prices, and as Arabs cultivated new customers. This made up for the temporary reduction in international tourism upon which the East Jerusalem economy depended. West Jerusalem became closer to everyone in East Jerusalem. They rode Israeli buses and taxis. They window shopped, frequented Israeli markets, and bought Israeli products. New relationships and new ventures began to evolve.

Although some Israelis knew Arabic, Hebrew became essential when navigating our new reality: speaking with new Israeli Jewish acquaintances, reading signs, listening to Israeli radio, dealing with Israeli bureaucracies. My second oldest sister, Anastasia, enrolled in Hebrew classes at the Convent of the Sisters of Zion, located near the eastern end of Via Dolorosa, and my oldest brother, Khamis, took a crash course in Hebrew at Ulpan Beit Ha'am in the western section of Jerusalem. Israeli female singer, Hadassah Sigalov, visited class to teach Hebrew through songs.

But the song that was heard everywhere was "Jerusalem of Gold."[55] As it bemoaned "The city that sits solitary // And in its midst is a wall," it ignored the inhabitants—us—on the other side of the wall. The lyrics, "Jerusalem of gold, and of bronze, and of light // Behold I am a violin for all your songs" would have been more meaningful had they been more inclusive, but we understood why. Part of the lyrical void was redressed some four years later when Fairuz, the beloved Christian Lebanese singer, released her album "Jerusalem in My Heart," containing songs like "*Zahrat El-Mada'en*" (Flower among Cities) and "*El-Quds Al-Atika*" (The Old City). Her voice echoed throughout our neighborhood and the eastern part of Jerusalem: "This is our home and Jerusalem belongs to us // And in our hands we will celebrate the splendor of Jerusalem // by our hands the peace will return to Jerusalem."[56]

Archeological digs were undertaken, and tourist locations were renovated. Holy places became holier, as Jews returned to the Western Wall after nineteen years of separation, and as pilgrims and tourists converged to see "where it all happened." Although holy sites are within each other's sights, there was not any overflowing of religious fervor toward the other. Jews visited and prayed at the Western Wall, Christians prayed along the Via Dolorosa and at the Church of the Holy Sepulchre, and Muslims prayed at Dome of the Rock and the Al-Aqsa Mosque.

While some Palestinians sought work in the eastern section of Jerusalem, more and more of them pursued their job searches inside Israel proper and its booming economy. The lower employment rate in the Palestinian areas, the high construction rate in Israel, and the higher Israeli pay—in contrast with Palestinian pay in East Jerusalem, the West Bank, or the Gaza Strip—induced, or even seduced, many to do so. Simultaneously, the price of goods rose, which was a serious disadvantage to those on fixed incomes—as was the case with my father, those who refused to work in Israel, or those who were beholden to the Jordanian government for their jobs, such as public officials and public school teachers.

It became harder to visit family and friends across the Jordan River. Israeli security subjected Palestinians, us included, to inordinate measures, disallowing electronics, toiletries, and printed or written materials. As Betty Dagher Majaj writes, "It was dehumanizing, humiliating, and terrifying. We were stripped naked and then had a metal detector passed over our naked bodies."[57]

As time progressed, most Palestinians—especially those living outside Jerusalem—had to tolerate daily security checks and sometimes recriminations and violence by both Israeli and Palestinian parties. These included some Israelis saying, "How can we trust you?" or "Why work here and take jobs away from us?" and some Palestinians saying, "How dare you work and benefit the enemy?" "Damned if you do and damned if you don't" became the oft-heard response.

A serious security issue expressed itself in the street below our garden. Samir, a neighbor, was arrested. Soon thereafter, his parents' two-story house was demolished. It took a long time for the stones to fall. We watched with deep concern and wondered what caused this collective punishment. Samir was sentenced to sixteen years in prison.

Returning to School

With the start of fall 1967, I began another year of schooling at Collège des Frères,[58] located next to the Old City's New Gate. Like Jaffa Gate and Zion Gate, this gate was blocked for nineteen years, as it faced no man's land. Instead of entering through Damascus Gate and making my way through the alleys and the marketplace, as was done before June 5, 1967, there was easy access after June 1967. Walking through the New Gate, I entered the school on the right, a major saving of effort and time.

The school, rubbing elbows with the Old City walls, had different spectators on the city ramparts than before June 1967. From class windows and the school playground, we no longer saw Jordanian soldiers on guard, but rather tourists armed with cameras circling the city from above and spectacular views and a mélange of sounds from inside and outside the wall. In short order, Israeli security patrols became visible near the New Gate and the other six open gates, atop Damascus Gate, and in the marketplace.

No teacher asked us—the students—to recount what we had done or been through during the summer. Perhaps it was because we all had undergone a similar trauma. Several students never returned; they must have transferred to other schools or left Jerusalem altogether. However, much was in the air. Continuity and change found varying expressions in each of us, as the school tried to keep us disciplined and focused.

Education was Arab in orientation with Western underpinnings. The teachers and administrators kept the Jordanian curriculum the same. They felt no need to introduce new requirements at that time. It was too soon to tell what would occur over the next months or years. Arabic and Arab history and literature, English and French, math and science, and Catholicism constituted the core. The Arab component assumed more emphasis than before June 1967. Whatever was presented, it was done within the context of the Arab national experience. Nothing was mentioned of Israel, Jews, or Hebrew, even though words like *shalom* (peace), *Shabbat* (Sabbath), and *Knesset* (Israeli parliament) entered the daily lexicon.

The school had excellent basketball and volleyball teams, with enough room for the teams to play. However, no space was available for soccer. On Saturdays, we accessed the playground at the Saint Clare Monastery, located near Abu Tor/Al-Thawri. It was an energizing experience as students competed, but we must have been noisy to the cloistered Poor Clare nuns! It was interesting as the students walked from and to the Old City through what used to be no man's land or West Jerusalem. That was the same way I usually traveled to and from school.

It was not all fun, especially for the seniors who studied hard to graduate and pass the *Tawjihi* (the general secondary examination of Jordan) or the GCE (the General Certificate of Education in the British Commonwealth). The latter was taken by those wishing to study in Europe, as opposed to studying in the West Bank, Jordan, or elsewhere around the Middle East.

If there were any general complaints from the students, they usually related to difficult homework or to uneasy conditions beyond the school's walls. I did not envy the administrators and teachers who seemed caught between a rock and a hard place. On the one hand, they wanted to be loyal to their educational mission; on the other hand, they had to deal with Palestinian aspirations and demands, and with Israeli policy or counter-policy. Their task became difficult, particularly during periods of demonstrations, riots, and strikes, when some of the students opted to boycott classes and fulfill their "national duty." The students' reaction was understandable. They just had been subjected to a traumatic experience not of their own making. Some of them objected to Jordanian rule, as they did to Israeli rule. They felt like second-class citizens in both. Alienated, angry, and frustrated, some of them took to the streets.

There was definite confusion and disillusionment. The lived reality in East Jerusalem and other territories Israel occupied did not cohere with the regional and international declarations. It seemed that the Arab rhetoric of the pre-June 1967 War continued after the war. Between August 29 and September 1, 1967, the leaders of several Arab countries met in Khartoum, Sudan, issuing the Khartoum Declaration,[59] which committed them to continue their fight against Israel and to maintain "the rights of the Palestinian people in their nation." Under Egypt's Abdel-Nasser's spell, they announced: "no peace with Israel, no negotiation with Israel, no recognition with Israel."

United Nations resolutions, while they provided a hopeful answer, always led to a dead end. On November 22, 1967, less than six months after the war, the UN Security Council adopted Resolution 242,[60] in which it specified the "inadmissibility of the acquisition of territory by war" and called for the "(i) Withdrawal of Israel armed forces from territories occupied in the recent conflict" and (ii) "Termination of all claims or states of belligerency and respect for and acknowledgment of the sovereignty, territorial integrity, and political independence of every State in the area and their right to live in peace within secure and recognized boundaries free from threats or acts of force."

These and other declarations sent people on a roller coaster ride. Some ignored them, calling them simply "ink on paper," while others saw in them the possibility of rebirth. My family and I learned fast how to navigate the labyrinths of the transforming reality in Jerusalem and put matters in proper perspective. However, there was always a certain level of uncertainty, even caution, about the world beyond—about the unknown around the corner.

3
FAMILY ROOTS

A seedling grows
not solely by its own
accord till sunlight caresses
its tiny leaves and massages
its green twigs, water
quenches its thirst, nutrients
feed its tender roots.

The wind above
embraces, the salty earth
below enfolds, for
without boundless knowledge,
without inordinate love,
life remains
blossomless, fruitless.

Our fight for survival, initial recovery from war, and adjustment to Israel's presence suddenly changed dimensions. It turned into a crisis of identity. Disbelief and doubt temporarily replaced fear. What we took for granted lost importance and meaning.

A few months after the war, while helping my parents around the house, my eldest brother, Khamis, came upon a long-held secret, at least for some of us children. He found a document written in an unfamiliar language. "That's nothing, nothing. Give it to me," my mother told my brother. Upon inspection and persistent questioning, my mother reluctantly explained that our father was not of Palestinian Arab heritage as we had thought all along. Similarly, she revealed that her own father was not fully of Palestinian Arab ethnic origin either.

It is hard to know why our parents did not tell us earlier about our grandparents' origins, especially our paternal grandfather. Perhaps they felt we were too young to understand and wanted to wait until we were more mature. Perhaps they were acting out of deference to our adoptive grandmother, who lived with us. Or, perhaps it was because the culture and society in which we lived did not fully embrace the idea of adoption, and not telling us was their way of protecting us.

Regardless, my whole life flashed before my eyes. Experiencing war and facing a new revelation brought survival and identity into stark view. Thoughts of being different crept into my mind; yet my new identity generated within me a new energy and a determination to survive. My desire to know the truth increased. Who am I? What are my parents' origins? If the wonderful lady who lived with us all these years is not my father's mother, as she indicated during the census, then *who* is she?

Undoubtedly, ancestry is essential to our identity and the meaning we make of our reality. While some are fortunate to know everything about their lineage, others are not. While some are content to live without knowledge of their familial roots, others do their best to discover them.

Unfortunately, I do not know everything about my parents' family backgrounds. My father's, though, is less defined than my mother's.

My Father: Prince or Pauper?

What is certain about my father is that he was Russian. His given name is Ivan, which is the Slavic equivalent of Johannes or John, or the Arabic equivalent of Hanna or Yuhanna.

There are several differing but related accounts that hint at Ivan's birth and formative years. The first is the family's account, told and retold for decades. It is based on what was originally stated by the Russian woman who cared for Ivan. He is described as a prince born in Saint Petersburg. While his father, a *dvoryanin* (a member of the czar's court), had to stay behind, my father was smuggled out of Russia to Palestine, specifically Jerusalem, by his mother to escape the turmoil besetting Russia at the time. The conflict eventually culminated in the two revolutions of March 1917 and November 1917.[61] The former led to the abdication of Czar Nicholas II, and the latter brought about Bolshevik rule and the czar's execution, along with that of members of his immediate imperial family. In addition, at least seventeen members of the ruling Romanov family were killed by the Bolsheviks, with the remaining thirty-five members taking refuge overseas, "narrowly managing to escape the same fate as their relatives."[62]

Why travel all the way to Palestine and Jerusalem, though? The answer finds itself decades after the Crimean War (October 1853-February 1856),[63] when Palestine in general—and its coastal cities on the Mediterranean, such as Jaffa and Haifa, in particular—witnessed major changes. Palestine's socioeconomic life became closely integrated into the world economy, revitalizing the cities which, in turn, witnessed robust economic growth accompanied by urbanization. Banking and credit systems, transportation and communication, industrial and handicraft production grew exponentially, impacting other spheres of life.[64] Aside from the natural increase in population, and the internal migration of people from the rural areas to the cities, there was a sizeable influx of European immigration, specifically Christian and Jewish.[65]

These changes impacted Jerusalem in a strong way: she no longer was deserted or overlooked. She took on a new life as Christians and Jews from Europe transformed her into a center of religious activity. Schools, hospitals, houses of worship, and charitable institutions were founded, which may have energized the local Arab Christian community. During the 1870s, pilgrims in the thousands began to flood Jerusalem. The city's development triggered "a construction boom that both signified and furthered the general economic expansion."[66]

Jerusalem's religious centrality was again highlighted and remains a favored destination—or even destiny—for Christians, as it was, and is, for other religious and ethnic communities. Christianity's holiest sites are in Bethlehem, the birthplace of Jesus Christ; in Nazareth, his home as a child and young man; and in Jerusalem, the location of his crucifixion, burial, and resurrection. In Jerusalem, the faithful weave the physical with the sacred—the outer world with the inner—to be nearer to Heaven and to find God.[67] In this sense, the act of pilgrimage or leaving for Jerusalem, as Ivan's mother or godmother did, embodied both secular and spiritual value meant to simultaneously protect the body and uplift the soul.

Russian pilgrims especially—often subsidized by the czarist government, but frequently using their life savings—came by tens of thousands, mainly during Christmas, New Year, and *Paskha* (Easter), with some of them walking the entire distance from Russia. Others arrived from the Black Sea ports by boat to the ancient port city of Jaffa on the Mediterranean Sea, and then made the difficult forty-one-mile (66 km) trek by foot or horse-drawn carriage to Jerusalem through the Bab el-Wad and the winding road up the steep hills. When the Jaffa-Jerusalem train was inaugurated in 1892, it became a preferred mode of transportation. Pilgrims then walked the short distance to the Old City.

During the early part of the 19th century, pilgrims found reasonable accommodations at Russian hostels in Palestine. By mid-century, the first Russian Ecclesiastical Mission, a private undertaking of the Russian Church, began providing a variety of services to pilgrims, including medical care and education to the Arab Orthodox inhabitants of Palestine and Syria. After the Crimean War, the mission was recognized by the Ottoman authorities, and it expanded its work in the Holy Land.[68] Subsequently, the Imperial Russian Orthodox Palestine Society—headed by Grand Duke Sergei Alexandrovitch (the brother of the ruling czar) from its headquarters in St. Petersburg—began construction on the *Maskobiyyeh*, or Russian Compound, 300 meters from the northwest corner of the Old City. This was done with the blessings of the Russian Czar and the financial services of Valero Bank.[69]

In time, the Russian Compound became a self-contained "hub," surrounded by a large stone wall. It consisted of a women's hospice, a men's hospice, residence for clergy and dignitaries, wells, a laundry facility, stables, chicken coops, and orchards with cypress, olive, and pine trees. The Holy Trinity Cathedral was beautiful inside and out, and its bells were heard throughout the city each afternoon and on holy days. A consulate handled the legal affairs and travel permits of both Russian residents and pilgrims.

Pilgrims frequented stores located on the ground floors of the Lord Bayyouk Building or adjacent buildings, local peddlers set up stalls at the nearby park or in the Holy City, and pilgrims bought food and souvenirs as they prepared to start their long-awaited spiritual journey. Business boomed around the Russian Compound. In the words of Wasif Jawhariyyeh, "It seemed as though a herd of black sheep was grazing up and down the street, one shopping, another praying and signing the cross. It was a beautiful sight, and the locals made a lot of money from those sheep."[70]

The pilgrims' deep faith led them to many religious sites: Church of the Nativity, River Jordan, Garden of Gethsemane, Church of the Holy Sepulchre, known to Eastern Christians as Anastasis or the Church of the Resurrection, Mount of Olives, Tomb of the Virgin, and Monastery of the Cross. Stephen Graham, the British journalist and travel-writer who accompanied Russian pilgrims in 1912, was both impressed and moved by them:

> "They sanctified crosses at the grave, little ones to wear round their necks in the tomb, and larger ones to lie on their breasts; they brought their death-shrouds and cross embroidered caps to dip them in Jordan; they took Jerusalem earth to put in their coffins, and even had their arms tattooed with the word Jerusalem, and with pictures of the Virgin; so that they might lie so marked in the grave, and indeed that they might rise again so marked, and show it in heaven."[71]

This first account of my father's background further explains that when four-year old Ivan arrived at the Russian Compound in Jerusalem, a concerted effort was undertaken to camouflage his true identity to protect him from evil-doers. The task of providing him with a new name, a new home, and a new life in the Holy City was entrusted to Tatiana, the wife of the general manager of the Russian Compound. My father called her "my caretaker," and "my guardian angel."

The second account gives Ivan more humble beginnings. His birthplace was at the government maternity hospital in the Russian Compound in Jerusalem. A baptismal certificate specifies September 16 (September 3, 1913 in the Julian calendar) as his birth date and September 20 (September 7, 1913 in Julian calendar) as his baptismal date. This account is largely based on a Russian Orthodox Church baptismal certificate, which was issued, or reissued, eighteen years after Ivan's birth. It names Daria Vasilievna Danilova as his mother, Mikhail Mikhailovich Mikhailov as his godfather, and Pelageya Abramovna Nikifirova as his godmother. No mention is made of his father. Officiating at the baptism was Ieromonah Tikhon (Hieromonk or Priestmonk Tikhon). Signing a copy of the 1913 baptismal certificate on September 11, 1931 in the Julian calendar (September 24, 1931 in the Gregorian calendar) was Ieromonah Afanasy, Acting Head of the Russian Orthodox Ecclesiastical Mission in Jerusalem.

If the family or first account is true, then the baptismal certificate is not, and Ieromonah Tikhon was an accomplice in fabricating a new identity for baby Ivan. If the baptismal certificate or second account is true, then what Tatiana said about Ivan's birth and background is not true. Moreover, if the baptismal certificate is authentic, then Ivan must not have been born in St. Petersburg. Otherwise, it would have necessitated a real miracle in those days of 1913 for Ivan to be born in Saint Petersburg on Tuesday and be baptized in Jerusalem on Saturday of the same week. The travel distance between the two cities is a mere 4,268 km (2,652 miles)!

Obviously, the two accounts raise other suggestions about Ivan's birth: given that there is no birth certificate to prove that Ivan was born in Saint Petersburg, could it be that his mother arrived pregnant from Russia? Baptizing Ivan four days after his birth is also intriguing. There must have been an urgent need to baptize him so quickly, such as a serious health emergency, considering that traditionally, babies are baptized on the eighth day or after. Moreover, neither account indicates anything about Ivan's care during the first four years of his life. The assumption is that his mother, or his godparents, would have been the ones to raise him. Godparenting is a great honor and carries an awesome responsibility. A main duty of godparents is to know the faith and provide guidance in accordance with the teachings of God; another is to assist the godchild in addressing whatever challenges might arise in life.

The outbreak of the First World War made Jerusalemites feel stranded. The environment in Jerusalem was extremely difficult: Western (e.g., Austrian, French, German, and Italian) presence diminished as the Ottoman Empire (that controlled the Holy Land for some four-hundred years, specifically during 1516-1917) became more aggressive toward the inhabitants. Western banks and post offices closed their doors. Lines of communication with the outside world were cut off. A locust invasion denuded the land of its vegetation during March-October 1915.[72] The Allies imposed a blockade of the coast; wheat became unavailable, which caused food rationing. Water was also rationed. Malnutrition and hunger became part of daily existence. Sanitation was almost nonexistent. Medicine was scarce; despair, disease, and death afflicted many residents; and some, especially children, died from typhus and other plagues. "At every level of society there was a sense that the entire world had turned against Jerusalem and Palestine."[73]

Regardless, there was the decision to find Ivan a home before his fifth birthday. Perhaps his mother or his godparents could no longer care for him. This matter became complicated and urgent by the events of the First World War and the Russian Revolutions and their aftermath. Russia and the Ottoman Empire fought on opposite sides of the war, with the former being a member of the Allied Powers, and the latter a member of the Central Powers. Following the Russian Revolution in October 1917, moreover, the Russian religious authorities became split between the Bolshevik or communist-backed Russian Orthodox Church, and those supportive of the Czarist tradition or the Russian Orthodox Church outside Russia.

Consequently, the flow of pilgrims dried up. Daily life at the Russian Compound and Russian convents elsewhere in Palestine became tough, even endangered. Ottoman soldiers occupied the Russian Compound and expelled the clergy and staff, as they did citizens of other countries who were fighting with the Allies against them. Russians in Jerusalem found themselves stranded without a financial, health, and social safety net. Those who did not return to Russia went temporarily to Egypt and were not allowed to return until 1919.

Whether the first or the second account is most accurate, I can picture my Russian grandparents discussing what is best for the family. I can see them agonizing over the tough but crucial decision to have the father stay in Russia, while the pregnant mother—or the mother with newborn Ivan—flee for relative safety in Jerusalem.

I can picture Ivan being born at the Russian Compound and the priest visiting him and his mother at the hospital on the day of the birth to read special prayers. I can picture baby Ivan's baptism: being carried into the *narthex* (entrance) of the Holy Trinity Cathedral; the godparents looking west to renounce Satan and then east to accept Jesus for the baby; the priest making the sign of the cross on the baby's body; the godparents reciting the Nicene Creed on the baby's behalf; the naked baby being cleansed by water in the baptismal font after being anointed with oil; the priest anointing the baptized baby with the Holy Chrism; dressing the baby in new clothes as if "putting on Christ;" circumambulating around the Font three times; the priest performing the tonsure or the cutting of four locks of hair from the baby's head in the form of the Cross; and finally, the baby receiving communion.

I can picture Ivan's godparents, and others of good will, helping Ivan's mother cope with a new reality: a baby, no father, no real support. I can picture Tatiana working with, or without, Ivan's mother, as well as with his godparents, to find Ivan the care and love he deserved. This was magnified in the minds of many Russians, as the news from back home was vague and increasingly unstable, and as conditions worsened for Russians in Jerusalem during the First World War.

An initial encounter to place Ivan with a family occurred in mid-1918, at a grocery store close to the Russian Compound. The Christian Arab owner, Mr. Fasheh, and his wife were desperate to have children of their own but could not. Tatiana shared her earnest wish with Mr. Fasheh, which resulted in Ivan spending the night with his family. My father remembered many tears being shed that night. No one or nothing could console him: strange adults, unfamiliar surroundings, a new language—all were too much to handle without the familiar assurance and a warm embrace. Moreover, Arab culture was not as receptive to the idea of adoption as it is today. It took much courage for couples at the time to adopt or go beyond guardianship. Alas, Ivan was returned to Tatiana the next morning.

Another encounter happened later that summer, probably in August 1918. This month stands out, as it coincided with the "falling asleep" or passing of the *Theotokos* (Mother of God)—her son, Jesus, receiving her soul, and the resurrection of her body three days later, as is believed in the Eastern Orthodox Church. My father recalled an enclosure packed with people and countless lit candles. In actuality, what he was describing was a religious ceremony taking place at the Tomb of the Virgin, or what Palestinian Christians call *Sitna Mariam*—a few yards from the Garden of Gethsemane with its old olive trees and a short walking distance from the Russian Orthodox Church of Mary Magdalene. The faithful, both clergy and laity—Arab, Greek, Russian, and other—filled the church's walled courtyard and down its forty-seven steps to Mary's tomb. Countless candles and dozens of votive lamps, icons and incense, the scent of basil and flowers, chanting and prayers enlivened the senses, the spirit.[74]

Tatiana and Ivan, in line for a while, finally made their way to the tomb. Ivan must have wandered and ended up pulling on a woman's dress, saying: "mama, mama, mama," thinking she was his mother. It was not long after that a friendly exchange occurred between Tatiana and the woman, who happened to be Maritza Zananiri, a Palestinian Christian from the Old City. "Where is his mother?" she asked. "His parents are dead," Tatiana answered. Unknown to Tatiana, Maritza had lost her two babies to typhoid[75] and was fervently praying for God's blessings and favor. Ivan descended "parentless" into the underground cave only to ascend into the light of hope and a better life to come. The pledge answered. A miracle, indeed!

The next day, Tatiana and Ivan arrived at the Zananiri house in the Masbaneh area of the Old City, part of what became the Christian Quarter under the British Mandate.[76] In addition to an ornate bed, the big box she had delivered contained mostly clothes, including a princely outfit with embroidery highlighted with gold thread and an equally decorative hat. With Tatiana and Maritza at his side, Ivan or Vanya (as Tatiana called him) was introduced to father Saba and a few other members of his new family.

Overnight, Ivan's world was turned upside down. He became known as Hanna Zananiri. His culture became Palestinian Christian, his main language Arabic. His religious denomination shifted from Russian Orthodox to Greek Orthodox. Although both denominations follow in Jesus's same footsteps, they do not always see eye-to-eye and are, at times, competitive. The extended family heard the good tidings, and Hanna was presented to the rest of the Zananiri family, as well as the Sarsar family. Sarsar is Maritza's maiden name, and she had an older brother, Khamis, and two younger sisters, Julia and Farideh. Khamis and his wife, Futun, lived nearby.

Hanna became attached to his "mother"—Maritza—and loved to hear his "father"—Saba—sing to him. He accompanied his "parents" to Mar Ya‍coub (Saint James)—the parish church of the Arabic-speaking Greek Orthodox community, adjacent to the Church of the Holy Sepulchre—and became fascinated from early age by the Orthodox liturgy and its melodic hymns.

Hanna was enrolled in the Schneller School to begin his kindergarten and primary education. Otherwise known as the Syrian Orphanage, the Schneller School was established by Johann Ludwig Schneller in Jerusalem in October 1860 and had both academic emphasis and vocational training, such as carpentry, engraving, farming, gardening, metalworking, painting, pottery, printing, shoemaking, and tailoring. It is there that Hanna improved his Arabic and learned some German. Except for a few words, Russian was forgotten. It is there that Hanna became familiar with basic Protestant religious teachings. It must have been somewhat confusing, to say the least, for Hanna to make sense of his changing, and often, contradictory reality.

At age nine, Hanna's world was turned upside down again. Two major events took place in his immediate surroundings, which altered his life forever.

The first had to do with Maritza's brother, Khamis, and her sister-in-law, Futun Hanna Kara‍a. Unable to have children of their own, Khamis and Futun adopted a child and named him Elias but then lost him to typhoid seven years later. This tragedy came soon after Maritza's and Khamis's brother Hanna who was conscripted into the Turkish army[77] died or disappeared during the First World War. No news was ever received from him or about him. Elias's death, like his uncle's, was heartbreaking for both the Sarsar and Zananiri families.

The second relates to the dire financial condition that faced most ordinary families during and after the First World War. Saba became unemployed and had a tough time providing for his family. Maritza, moreover, was expecting a baby, after having lost two of her own children.

Out of both sympathy and empathy, and out of family and financial concerns, a decision was made to have Hanna move in with the Sarsars. Even though the new environment was more familiar to Hanna than when he first arrived to live with the Zananiris, I cannot imagine the effect this decision had on all concerned, especially Maritza and Hanna—Maritza having raised Hanna for four years and then having to give him up, and Hanna feeling tossed around as if no one cared.

People did care, however. Maritza was doing a good deed and could see Hanna any time she wanted. Hanna did not lose another "father" and "mother." He gained new ones.

While this fateful decision appeared sensible, it was a shock for Tatiana. When she found out about it, she was profoundly upset. The decision was made without her knowledge, without consultation. She asked to take Ivan, or Hanna, back. It took a long time to convince her otherwise. It took a long time for her to calm down and agree to the new arrangement.

As planned, Hanna moved in with the Sarsars, but his name was changed, *again*—this time to George. Khamis and Futun were reluctant to keep the name Hanna, as Khamis's brother, Hanna, never returned home during the First World War. To ward off another bad omen, they chose instead the name George, which is a favored name in the Palestinian Christian community. The original George, Greek by birth, was a Roman soldier who lived in Lydda, Palestine in the 3rd century CE. Martyred in 303 during Emperor Diocletian's persecutions, he later became a saint venerated in many cultures.

As envisioned, Hanna/George developed a close friendship with the Zananiri family. He and his Zananiri "parents" visited each other regularly. He and the Zananiri children—Issa, Elaine, and Tawfiq who were born after Hanna/George moved with the Sarsars—became good friends. His eyes would light up as he repeated to us circular stories he used to tell Tawfiq, but Tawfiq was rarely pleased, as these stories had no satisfactory ending to them. Tawfiq, unfortunately, died young.

The main responsibility for raising George was in Khamis and Futun Sarsar's hands, but more so in Futun's as time progressed. Khamis and Futun lived in the Old City, a short distance from Damascus Gate, in what they and others referred to as Haret al-Haddadeen (the blacksmiths' neighborhood). Their house, with its ultimate title held by the Greek Orthodox Patriarchate of Jerusalem—the largest non-governmental property owner in the Holy Land—was in Dar el-ᶜItmeh (the abode of darkness). They called it as such because of its dirt, long-sloping, downward entrance that was pitch black regardless of the time of day and night (until a light bulb was installed decades later), but eventually led to a sunny courtyard and a three-level house. They had a living room, two bedrooms, and a kitchen, and shared the use of a stable, a well, and a squat toilet with two other families who lived in the same housing compound.

George was taken out of Schneller and enrolled in the free school at Collège des Frères, which consisted of only six elementary classes. The other parallel school, as described by Issa J. Boullata, who attended the school a couple decades after George, consisted of "seven elementary classes and four secondary ones; it had another team of teachers and charged school fees—rather steep ones."[78] This Roman Catholic school, adjacent to the New Gate, was a few minutes' walk from home through Al-Gabsha St. to St. Francis St., past St. Saviors Convent on the right, and up the bend to the large metal gate.

Since its founding by the La Salle Brothers in 1876, Collège des Frères has educated students regardless of their religious affiliation or national identity. The order of classes when my father studied there followed the French educational system, so that the lowest class was the fifth, and the highest class was the first. The intensity and quality of education were high, as was the number of students who studied there.

George, a Russian boy—raised by his second set of Palestinian Christian parents, and a member of the Greek Orthodox Church—was studying at a Roman Catholic institution that highlighted French culture!

Even though he adjusted well to school, his attendance was uneven. Part of the reason had to do with his father, Khamis.

Khamis Sarsar was born in Jerusalem in 1887. He is the son of Salim ᶜAbdo and Farideh Khashram. Handsome, tall, and well-groomed, he wore a *tarboush*, or fez, which endowed him with an air of charisma and maturity beyond his years. His curved moustache, which surpassed the sultan's, at times gave him a stern look. Women often hung around by their doors or windows to gaze at him as he walked to and from work.

Khamis Sarsar's name was, in reality, Khamis ᶜAbdo. The name change evolved because he used to hang around and work closely with his maternal uncles, the Sarsars, which led most people to call him Khamis ᶜAbdo Sarsar. ᶜAbdo Sarsar is actually the official family name in the Greek Orthodox Church registry.[79] Over time, only the name Sarsar was retained.

Khamis was a master barber. He and a partner, Mr. Mallouk, opened a barbershop in the Old City at today's intersection of Christian Quarter Street and Al-Khanqa Ascent. Work was usually slow on Mondays through Fridays but brisk on Saturdays and Sundays. The cost for customers was little, even by the living standards of those days: a haircut was four piasters; a shave, two piasters; a combination of a haircut and a shave, five piasters.

Following the loss of his brother, Hanna, during the First World War and the death of his adopted son, Elias, soon thereafter, Khamis's pain was overwhelming. He became depressed and found comfort in alcohol and tobacco. His addictions cost him and his family dearly in the long run. While the prices of goods and services were low, it became extremely hard to pay for *Arak* (a licorice-flavored alcohol) and cigarettes and maintain a good, let alone healthy, living.

Young George often stopped by the barbershop on the way back from school to lend a hand: sweep the floor, make order, and go on small errands. It reached a point when Khamis began to take his son out of school in order to be "the barber's assistant." That made it easier on him to frequent the nearby café to drink and play cards or backgammon with his friends. When a customer arrived for a haircut or shave, George ran to fetch him.

One day, a customer by the name of Nicola Khoury—Principal of Al-Madrassah Al-Wataniyyeh (National School), located at the Nusseibeh family property in Musrara—came in for a haircut. Upon inquiring why George was not in school, he took a strong stand and convinced Khamis to straighten his ways and promise not to let George miss school again. Henceforth, George was enrolled in the National School. In later years, Nicola was ordained and became Abouna Nicola, the parish priest of the Greek Orthodox Church.

When not in school, and when work was slow at the barbershop, George was wise at an early age to use the time to do his homework or just read. One of the regular customers saw potential in him and bought him books on a variety of topics, provided he agreed to read them and give a summary of each when the customer returned for his haircuts. Without a high school diploma or a college degree, George became an avid reader, passionate about history and literature. He devoured biographies, stories of heroism, travelogues, and even poetry. He loved to recite short poems whenever an appropriate occasion presented itself.

George did his best to help his parents overcome some of the challenges they faced. As he entered adolescence, he took on several jobs, including working at another barbershop (owned by an Armenian) in the same vicinity and house painting. However, his love of reading naturally led him to love the alphabets and the formation of words even more. He became familiar with various languages and was, by the age of sixteen, able to put them to good use. No, he did not become a writer, a translator, or a journalist, but rather a typesetter. His first typesetting job was at the Greek Orthodox Patriarchal Printing Press, part of the Greek Orthodox Patriarchate in Jerusalem. The press is the oldest in the Holy Land, founded by Patriarch Kyrill II in 1853.

Also at age sixteen, George became exceedingly interested in learning more about his Russian family roots. Wanting to reassure George and solidify their parental connection, Khamis and Futun took him to the Church of the Holy Sepulchre, where they prayed and lit candles at Calvary and the Tomb of Christ. They then proceeded to the parish church of Mar Ya'coub next door and formally adopted him. Abouna Ghorghori Khamis officiated at the religious ceremony, telling George while pointing in turn to each of Futun and George, "This is your mother. This is your father. These are your parents now. You are their son!"

At age eighteen, George visited the Church of Saint Alexander Nevsky (named after the 13th-century Russian warrior-prince), located a short distance from the Church of the Holy Sepulchre. It is there that he filed a formal request with the Russian Church administration for his baptismal certificate. It is unclear if Tatiana encouraged him to do so or not.

My Mother: Motherless But Deeply Loved

My mother's background is found in the union of the Korfiatis and Karaʿa families. The former is Greek, and the latter is Palestinian Arab.

The Korfiatis family has lived in Jerusalem for over one-hundred-seventy-five years. Like others before and after them, the Korfiatises immigrated to the Holy Land due to a variety of hardships at home, or perhaps because they saw potential in greener pastures beyond their homeland as they searched for religious worth, economic opportunity, ethnic belonging, and even adventure.

Historically, Greek and Arab Orthodox Christians felt at home in the Holy Land. Along with other Orthodox Christians (Albanians, Bulgarians, Georgians, Serbs, and Vlachs), the Ottoman Empire granted them a semi-autonomous status as *millet-i Rûm* (Roman or Byzantine nation). Greek Orthodox churches dotted the land. The Greek Orthodox Patriarchate, through the faithful and its landed property, enjoyed great financial and political influence.[80] Greeks worshipped on Sunday and holy days and worked the rest of the time on church-related projects or in the communities where they lived, which were mostly Palestinian Arab. They generally felt close to Palestinian Christians and Palestinian culture in terms of foods, music, and dance, among other things. Some Greek men were happy to marry Palestinian Christian women.

The original home of the Korfiatis family is Corfu, an island in the Ionian Sea. Their initial name is Triantáfyllo, meaning rose. As they originated from Corfu, people know them as Corfiatis or Korfiatis, and that how their name stuck.

The Korfiatis family traces its beginnings to Nicolaos Korfiatis and his son, Dimitrios. Georgios, the grandson, born in Corfu in 1812, must have visited Jerusalem as a young adult, was impressed by what he saw, and stayed. He married into the Khayyat family and had a son, Damianou, who was born in Jerusalem in 1840. In time, Damianou married Jamilah Munayyer and had five children: Sarah (1879), Zoe (1881), Sophia (1883), Frosso (1884), and George (1885). Each of them married into a Palestinian Arab family. George, specifically, first married Nazar George Al-Fahel and had three sons from her: Jani (1903), Wadie^c (1906), and Anton (1909). He then married Hanneh Daoud Al-Shama^c and had one son: Elias (1920).

As if it were not enough that the original family name was changed from Triantáfyllo to Korfiatis, another name began to be used. Many in the Palestinian community started calling them by the name Zayer (Arabic for visitor). Moreover, the father and sons became masonry and painting contractors, and took on major jobs in Jerusalem and adjacent locales.

It is Jani George Korfiatis (or Jamil Zayer) who married into the Kara^ca family. It is the same family of Futun, Khamis Sarsar's wife.

Futun is the daughter of Hanna Kara^ca and Mariam Zahra, and has two sisters, Julia and Anastasia. The Kara^cas originated from the town of Bethlehem, some six miles (10 km) south of Jerusalem, and the Zahras are from Jerusalem.

Hanna, Futun's father, was a master mason. One of his main accomplishments, according to Futun, was assisting the Greek monks in their construction of several buildings in the Old City, and the reconstruction of the Greek Orthodox Monastery at Jebel Quarantel or Mount of Temptations that rises behind old Jericho. This work was done during the latter part of the 19th century. The monastery clings to the eastern face of the mountain, viewed by many as the site where Christ was tempted three times by the devil during his forty-day fast.

Mariam Zahra Kara^ca was widowed at an early age. She had to raise her three young daughters, all born in Jerusalem, on her own. They followed in her footsteps in the way they behaved and dressed: always lady-like and proper. While Mariam continued to earn a living by decorating Palestinian men's and women's simple, loose attires with gold and silver thread, Julia, Futun, and Anastasia learned how to embroider. They became part of the embroidery community set up by Mrs. Bertha

Spafford Vester,[81] who helped women and girls to make money by selling their handicrafts in the United States.

Julia, the oldest daughter, was born in the first part of the 1890s. Accommodating, generous, and good-natured, she provided great support for her mother and served as a role model for her younger sisters. In her late teens, she married Nicola Nasser Mukhar, a young carpenter from Jerusalem and over a twelve-year period had five children. While Nicola worked closely with Mrs. Vester on many of her American Colony projects, Julia focused her full attention on raising her children. Like several Jerusalem families, the Mukhar family moved from inside the Old City to the Musrara neighborhood, a short walk outside the Damascus Gate. Musrara was started in the late 19th century by Palestinian Arab families, many among them Christian. They felt the need to be liberated from overcrowding within the walls.

Futun was the second daughter. She told me that her mother told her she was born the day of the blizzard at the start of the 20th century. She was shorter than Khamis, and her plump face and mild smile conveyed kindness. She was capable and dependable and, when necessary, tough. Between her birth and her death, Futun had a tough life, always putting the interests of others ahead of her own. The family challenges were huge, not to mention the uncontrollable crises beyond the home. First, there came the adoption of Elias and his untimely death. Second, there was the adoption of my father, George.

Anastasia was the youngest daughter. Born in 1904, she, like her sisters became an embroiderer. She loved to dress up and be fashionable. On Sunday, January 25, 1925, she married Jani George Korfiatis, a handyman/painter who did not make much money in those days. Jani and Anastasia moved into a modest house in Musrara, consisting of a small bedroom/living room, a tiny kitchen, a squat toilet, and a stone courtyard with potted plants. This is in contrast to several palatial houses in the neighborhood, which had shingled roofs, magnificent entrances, adorned façades, impressive masonry, arched windows, and tiled floors.

On January 4, 1926, with the assistance of a midwife, Anastasia gave birth at her home to baby Evelyn. Evelyn became the center of attention and was loved not only by her parents, but equally by her grandmother, Mariam, and her two aunts, Julia and Futun, and their families.

Everyone in the family always remembered Evelyn's baby years, but not because she was vivacious. Something more energetic and destructive occurred when Evelyn was only one and a half years old. On July 11, 1927, a major earthquake, with its epicenter located south of the Dead Sea and measuring 6.3 M_w, hit the region. Several cities in Palestine and in Transjordan were seriously affected.[82] In Jerusalem, around one-hundred-thirty people were killed, and four-hundred-fifty were injured. Some three hundred houses and other structures were damaged, including the domes of the Al-Aqsa Mosque and the Church of the Holy Sepulchre. Many families, like the Sarsars and Mukhars, spent that night in the open air, fearing another earthquake or aftershock.

Two years later, Anastasia gave birth to baby George but lost her life soon after the delivery. Birth complications, mainly excessive bleeding that could not be stopped, led to this shocking tragedy. If anything, it speaks volumes of the poor financial and health conditions that existed at that time. Many a wife (sometimes with prodding from husbands) preferred to stay home and have a midwife help in the delivery, rather than ending up with huge hospital bills.

Following a short service at Mar Ya‘coub, Jani Korfiatis, Nicola Nasser Mukhar, Khamis Sarsar, sixteen-year old George Sarsar, and others carried Anastasia's open coffin on the tips of their fingers through Christian Quarter Road, Bab el-Khalil (Jaffa Gate), and up the northern ascent of Mount Zion to the Greek Orthodox Cemetery. Jerusalem residents, shopkeepers, and tourists watched the funeral procession pass by, with Anastasia in her wedding dress decorated with carnations and roses. She was buried close to the cemetery's entrance, on the left side of the narrow walkway.

Anastasia's passing turned Jani into a widower and left Evelyn and George motherless. Mariam stepped in and volunteered to care for both of them. Jani agreed only to let Evelyn remain with her grandmother as "a compensation for her mother," but not George. Mariam and Evelyn then moved down the alley to live with her daughter, Julia, and the Mukhar family.

The Mukhar family consisted of Julia, her husband, Nicola, their three daughters (Labibeh, Nabiha, and Mary) and two sons (Nasser and Hanna). Their house was spacious with four rooms: the first for Julia and

Nicola, the second for the three daughters, the third for the two sons, and the fourth for Mariam and Evelyn. They shared a kitchen, a squat toilet, and a small courtyard that opened into a 7x15 meter garden, rich with fruit trees and vegetables. Nicola's two sisters, Zahieh and Katbeh, in addition to the Mansour family, were immediate neighbors. Along with her mother, Julia took care of her niece, Evelyn. In fact, she breastfed her, as she was breastfeeding her own son, Hanna, who was of the same age. Evelyn had great playmates and lifelong friendships with her "sisters and brothers," the five Mukhar children.

Within a few weeks of his wife's passing, Jani paid a visit to the Mukhar family. In addition to Mariam and Evelyn, Julia, Nicola, and Futun were also present. The visit was not social or to check on Evelyn's wellbeing; it was financial. Jani asked to see and have his wife's jewelry. "How dare you walk into my house," Nicola said in disbelief, "and make such a request?" "If it indicates anything," he stated angrily, "it is *waqaha*" (shameless audacity). Futun added, "You know, Anastasia worked so hard to buy this jewelry. Part of it was our wedding gift for her. It is now Evelyn's and baby George's." Jani explained, "I understand, and Evelyn and George are my children. As you know, Anastasia and I bought a piece of land near San Simon (the Greek Orthodox St. Simeon Monastery) in Katamon,[83] and I need the jewelry to build a small house on it." Julia interrupted, "You mean Anastasia bought the land."[84] Mariam, with Evelyn on her lap, broke her silence: "The precious life is gone. Am I going to worry about material stuff, even though it is gold? Give him the jewelry; all of it." She continued, "Jani, I do not want to see your face again!" Before leaving with the jewelry box, Jani promised to give Evelyn her fair share when she grew up.

It was not long afterwards that Jani placed baby George at a convent, got married to Louisa Yaᶜcoub Kafᶜity, and began building his house in Katamon. Unfortunately, it was reported that George was struck by pneumonia and passed away a few months after his mother. However, Jani never provided the convent's name. No funeral arrangements were made. No one knows where he was buried. Did George truly die, or was he put up for adoption? Why did not Jani and his wife, Louisa, raise George? These questions were never answered.

Regardless, George was gone. I cannot imagine how Mariam, Julia, and Futun must have felt when they heard the sad news: devastation, certainly, if not a strong sense of guilt. Why did not they insist on keeping George with them? What if George and Evelyn grew up together? Their lives would have been different, with George a solid anchor for Evelyn!

If Anastasia's passing and Jani's less than positive attitude were not enough, Khamis's health deteriorated. The barbershop was sold to his partner for little money, and his income stopped. Financially, it became extremely hard to cope.

Conditions between Arabs and Jews in Jerusalem and the surroundings became more charged than usual during the 1920s. With the British in charge, this decade witnessed the Jerusalem or Nabi Musa riots in April 1920, Arab general strikes in November 1925 and in March 1926, respectively, and major violence in late August 1929. These serious disturbances complicated matters for the inhabitants of Jerusalem and made all cautious as to whom they interacted with, where they worked, and where they shopped. They became the precursors of more difficult years and decades to come. The inhabitants, my family included, learned how to roll with the punches in order to survive. Their ordinary days were tough. Their sorrows were intense. Their happiness was never complete.

4
PARENTS' WEDDING

There was no choir, no music
but smiles of relief, of satisfaction.
Family and friends watched
years of pain and toil of
the older generation wash away,
birthing sure steps of
the young toward matrimony,

toward parenthood, and
a life of less pain and toil
in the land called holy.
The dove has yet to deliver
the olive twig, to set free
the mind from needless fright,
the heart toward a joyful silence.

The tensions between Palestinian Arabs and Jews, which have simmered since the start of the 20th century, erupted into outright violence during the British Mandate, which was formally confirmed by the Council of the League of Nations on July 24, 1922, and which entered into effect on September 29, 1923. If anything, the mandate made Palestinian Arab-Jewish relations worse: increased Jewish immigration, especially from Russia and Eastern Europe; large land purchases by Jews, primarily from absentee Arab landlords; Jewish settlements and a separate Jewish labor, as facilitated by the British economic policy; and the perceived divide and rule policies of the British—all eventually led to demands, riots, and a few major violent episodes.

One tragic incident related to the Wailing Wall. A disagreement over the site started in September 1928, "when Jewish worshippers brought items for prayer to the Wailing Wall that Muslims deemed to exceed the norm established during the Ottoman period. Upon Muslim complaint, the British police took action, and Jews responded strongly with protest, demonstration, strike, and mob action."[85] Accusations and demonstrations spilled over to 1929, when they led to outright inter-communal aggression. Arab losses reached three-hundred dead and fifteen-hundred wounded, and those of the Jews and the British armed forces one-hundred-thirty dead and two-hundred-forty wounded.[86] Then, the Palestinian Arabs killed fifty-nine Jews in Hebron.

This episode poisoned the connections between Palestinian Arabs and Jews for years. It "generated a process of rapid social, geographical, and political separation between the two rival political communities whose relations came to assume an increasingly hostile nature."[87] The British followed up by sending the first of several royal investigative commissions.[88]

Futun Sarsar persevered during this inter-communal upheaval and through her family's hardships; she had no choice. She sought employment, in addition to the beautiful embroidery she did for the American Colony. Luckily, she secured work as housekeeper at the Swedish School (Svenska Skolan or Madraset el-Assouj), a prominent primary school, located in a mixed Arab-Jewish quarter in the Musrara neighborhood, not far from Damascus Gate. Founded in 1902, it was owned and directed by the (Lutheran) Swedish Jerusalem Society. This position was great, as it provided a salary for Futun and room and board for her, her husband, Khamis, and young George.

Futun's presence at the school was most rewarding, personally and communally. Signe Ekblad—the headmistress whose presence at the school since 1922 enabled miracles to happen for her needy Arab female students—and Futun became work partners. In addition to being a dedicated educator, a socially responsible leader, and an empathetic social worker, Ekblad befriended her staff and treated each, including Futun, with equality. "These qualities were central in the ideology of the settlement movement and Ekblad's years at Birkagården, where equality among people regardless of class, race, and gender were essential ideals, and should not be underestimated as a fundamental influence on her relations with her staff in Jerusalem."[89]

As Khamis's medical condition worsened, doctors prescribed stronger medicine. While some suggested bedrest, others recommended a long sojourn to the historic city of al-Khalil, Hebron, located nineteen miles (30 km) south of Jerusalem, and rising 3,050 feet (930 meters) above sea level, where the air was supposedly cleaner than in other locales. The trip was taken, but to no avail: his liver and lungs stopped functioning properly.

Futun was deeply in love with Khamis and stood by his side through thick and thin. When he died, there was a large procession. The horse-drawn carriage bore his coffin down Jaffa Road, passing in front of the Russian Compound and Jaffa Gate, to his final resting place at the Greek Orthodox Cemetery on Mt. Zion. He was buried on the right side of the cemetery's main path, a few yards from Anastasia. Futun had a brownish, decorative Italian marble placed atop his grave. She mourned for decades, wearing only dark clothes—under-garments and all.

With Khamis's passing in 1935, Mariam Zahra Kara'a and Evelyn Korfiatis moved from the Mukhar family to live with Futun and George at the Swedish School. While twenty-one-year-old George continued his work at the Greek Orthodox Patriarchal Printing Press, nine-year old Evelyn started her fourth year at the Swedish School, but this time, she was the only student in residence! A year later, Futun learned from the Mukhar family that Sara Mitri Katan was selling her three-room house with a garden in Al-Thawri, the hill to the south of the Jaffa Gate and

Mount Zion. With monies saved, Futun bought the modest dwelling for 200 *junayh filastini* or Palestinian pounds on January 13, 1937, rented it immediately to the Sruji family, and began earning a monthly income.

As life became more routine and stable for Futun and her family at the Swedish School, it deteriorated in Palestine and became even more dangerous. Tensions between Palestinian Arabs and Jews flared up again, resulting in the generalized Palestinian Arab rebellion against the British and the Zionists during 1936-1939, and additional British commissions and reports.[90] "The root causes of the revolt remained unchanged: the Arab Palestinians' antipathy toward pro-Zionist British policies and their inability to advance toward self-rule."[91] Political protests and strikes led to attacks and retaliations. Palestinian Arabs boycotted Jewish businesses and stopped cooperating with the British. Lawlessness raged. Infighting between traditional Palestinian Arab notables and lower socioeconomic classes, or the grassroots, ensued. The insurgents among them "not only targeted British and Zionist interests but also attacked the privileged classes of Palestinians, obliging wealthy Palestinians to 'donate' to the nationalist cause…The Palestinian economy was devastated by the rebellion and especially by the anarchy and criminality that became so prominent in its last stages."[92]

With major reinforcements, the British Mandate authorities quelled the rebellion, brutally. It engaged in human rights abuses and devastated the Arab Palestinian leadership.[93] The cost was exceedingly high, and the record was long with imprisonment, exile, assassinations, atrocities, torture, and destruction of villages. Aside from hundreds of Jews and Britons killed or wounded, there were 5,000 Palestinians killed, 15,000 wounded, and 5,600 incarcerated.[94]

The British legitimized their counterinsurgency campaign through legal means. As Matthew Hughes argues, "The law was (re)constructed to provide a veneer of legal respectability to actions carried out by servicemen operating in the field against Arab rebels…."[95] The high cost of the Palestinian Arab Revolt did not end there. It became the ember that lit the next conflagration between Palestinian Arabs and Jews less than a decade later. "The Revolt was the prelude to what increasingly became an inevitable all-out war between Jews and Arabs for the exclusive ownership of Palestine."[96]

Futun, Mariam, George, and young Evelyn, like all others, had to survive. That took precedence over any national or political fervor. Their errands, their comings and goings, subjected them to all kinds of dangers. The newspaper coverage of the rebellion and the tragic stories they heard must have worried them. It is a miracle that they were not harmed. Being at the Swedish School provided them with a sense of normalcy and with refuge away from the blood, insecurity, and pain besetting Jerusalem and beyond.

Leul Ras Kassa Hailu and his family moved into the Halaby house next door to the Swedish School, and Futun, Mariam, George, and Evelyn became friends with them. Ras (Prince) Kassa, as they affectionately called him, was the trusted advisor and confident of Emperor Haile Selassie of Abyssinia (Ethiopia). In 1936, he, his wife, Princess Tsige Mariam Besha of Merhabete, and their fourteen-year-old son, Asrate, accompanied the Emperor into exile in Jerusalem, following invasion of Abyssinia by fascist Italy in 1935-36. Escaping violence and defeat in Abyssinia, they arrived into Mandated Palestine's violent environment. Their sojourn in Jerusalem extended until 1941, when they returned to Ethiopia during the East African Campaign and helped liberate the country. Ras Kassa became "the Emperor's longest serving president of his Crown Council, and was regarded as the most powerful figure in the Empire next to the monarch himself."[97] Following his death, Prince Asrate Kassa became Viceroy of the Province of Eritrea and head of the Selalle line of the Shewan wing of Ethiopia's Solomonic Dynasty.

A direct impact of the Palestinian Arab Revolt on Futun, Mariam, George, and Evelyn was the disruption to George's work. His full-time employment at the Greek Orthodox Patriarchal Printing Press turned to part-time, reducing his meager salary to almost nothing. He worked every other week and received three dinars per week. Futun's salary, rental income, and ability to manage saved the day.

In the meantime, the Second World War heated up, subjecting millions of Jews and others to the Holocaust.[98] These events—both criminal and extremely tragic—were far from Jerusalem. While generating empathy, they did not directly affect the daily lives of ordinary people, like Evelyn and George, at that time.

Evelyn Korfiatis and George Sarsar

Evelyn did her elementary education at the Swedish School. She was studious and loved learning from her teachers—Hana ᶜAbla, Wardeh Abu Dayyeh, Linda Farradj, Nabiha Halabi, and Badiᶜa Harami—whom she remembered with great fondness decades later. One time, when she got seriously ill with the flu, she missed two weeks of school. Her grades suffered during that marking period, dropping her to second place, which caused her "to cry and cry." That did not last long, however, as she graduated from sixth grade at the top of her class.

Evelyn was then enrolled at Al Ma'mouniyya School for Girls, close to the Old City's Herod's Gate. There, she was first in her class as well, earning the highest grades in English and mathematics. She graduated from eighth grade with high honors. Her goal was to pursue a higher degree and become an architect, as she often attempted to design and build things. This never materialized, as extra funds were nonexistent and as other family plans impacted her life.

Evelyn was proactive from an early age. She sought the outdoors. Sometimes, that came at a high price. In kindergarten, as she was building a sand castle, a classmate pushed her from behind and she fell on sand and all, cutting her tongue. It was painful, taking weeks to heal.

Evelyn was also competitive and participated in sports activities. She was basketball team captain and shooter and, with her team, often competed against the teams of other schools. She was also a runner. Once, as she was winning the tournament and ready to cross the finish line, another student, Fatima, less than a yard away from her, caught her by the uniform, leading her to fall on her face and break most of her teeth, especially the upper ones. While Fatima was reprimanded by the coach and school principal, a dentist in Ramallah restored Evelyn's front teeth and supposedly used gold to fill her back teeth. This dental procedure would subsequently cause a major medical emergency in later years.

Although still a teenager, Evelyn was developing into a beautiful, educated, and mature "young lady." As soon as she completed Al Ma'mouniyya, her father Jani showed up and wanted to take her back. Mariam and Futun intensely objected. They literally stood in his way, arguing that what he was asking for was contrary to the agreement they had after Anastasia's passing—mainly that Mariam would raise Evelyn.

While perhaps taboo in other societies, a discussion arose about twenty-eight-year-old George getting engaged to fifteen-year old Evelyn. Falling in love and motherhood were the farthest things from Evelyn's mind. Futun, fearing that Jani might return with a court order for his daughter's return, encouraged George to speak with Jani and ask for Evelyn's hand in marriage. George followed up, but was rebuffed immediately. Jani's relationship with Mariam and Futun was not so great; George was almost twice Evelyn's age, and George, in his eyes, was not well-off. Upon hearing about his son's objection to the engagement, George Damianou Korfiatis stepped forward and gave his permission. George Damianou loved his granddaughter, and since she and her grandmother, Mariam, did not object, he consented. He, in fact, officiated at the engagement ceremony.

Like other girls and boys in those days, Evelyn skipped adolescence. While engaged for one year, she began to focus more and more on George as her future husband. She and George often took strolls around Jerusalem. They accompanied Mariam and Futun to church on Sunday mornings. They occasionally took day trips to towns outside Jerusalem, including Bethlehem and Ramallah. Jericho was a favorite of theirs, as they visited Qasr Hisham (Hisham's Palace), an early Islamic archaeological site, and St. George's Monastery in Wadi Qelt, and as they immersed their feet in the River Jordan and the salty waters of the Dead Sea.

Evelyn attended a six-month sewing workshop, given by Kukon Tleel at the YW (Young Women's Christian Association) in the Mamilla neighborhood of Jerusalem and, in time, became an expert seamstress. She used Futun's Singer hand-crank sewing machine to make several of her dresses. She learned to do all kinds of household chores. With her grandmother and aunt, she cooked elaborate Middle East dishes, ranging from *hummus* and *tabbouleh* salad to *mejadra* (lentils dish) and stuffed grape leaves. She baked bread. She made sweets and desserts, such as *kaek wa maʿmoul* (stuffed cookies with dates and nuts) and *helbeh* (fenugreek cake).

Closer to their wedding day, Evelyn and George went on a shopping spree, even though their savings were at rock bottom. Their first stop was

Al-Maghasan jewelry store on Salah e-Din Street, where they bought their 22k gold rings. Their second stop was Dar al-Aytam al-Islamiyya (Islamic Orphan House) in the Old City, where they ordered shiny, solid, hand-made furniture for the reception room or salon (four single arm chairs, two double sofas, and four small coffee tables) and for the bedroom (two queen beds joined together, two nightstands, a four-door armoire, and a large two-piece vanity with a semi-rounded mirror). After returning home, Evelyn visited her girlfriend, Marguerite Mansour, who was getting married in a few weeks. She heard much about Marguerite's wedding dress and wanted to see it and feel it!

Evelyn and George's wedding ceremony was modest but elegant. It took place on Sunday, June 7, 1942. Wearing an A-line wedding gown with vintage buttons running down the front, a matching short sleeve jacket, and a two-tier chapel length lace edge veil,[99] Evelyn walked into the hall at the Swedish School with George, who was dressed in a double-breasted suit with lemon blossoms decorating the left lapel.

In addition to the bride and groom, those present included Father Khalil Hakim, the parish priest of the Arabic-speaking Greek Orthodox community, Mariam, Futun, the Mukhar family, Marguerite, and Signe Ekblad and her assistant, Ms. Svenson. Nasser Mukhar was the best man, and Mary Mukhar the bridesmaid. While Nasser wore a navy suit, Mary had a sky-blue long dress. This contrasted with Mariam and Futun, who had dark long dresses on—the former still in mourning for her daughter, Anastasia, after twelve years, and the latter still in mourning for her husband, Khamis, after seven years. David ᶜAbdo was the official photographer. Missing was Jani who never received an invitation.

Evelyn and George stood before Jesus Christ through the parish priest and the wedding company, expressing their commitment to God and to each other.[100] There was no exchange of vows, but rather prayers for God's blessings upon the rings and their placement on the ring fingers of George and Evelyn. The two wedding crowns, blessed and connected by a white ribbon, were placed on their heads, symbolizing their union and confirming their role as King and Queen of their household. After sipping wine from the "common cup," they followed the priest as he circled the table three times, holding the Gospel and the Cross.

As soon as the priest removed the crowns, George and Evelyn joined their family and friends at a simple reception of cake and soft drinks. Futun made sure to give Evelyn her four 22k gold bracelets, which she herself received from Mariam when she got married to Khamis Sarsar. This wedding gift was the only one Evelyn received that afternoon, but it was most precious, as Evelyn fully understood the intergenerational love, meaning, and symbolism the bracelets held.

George and Evelyn Sarsar bid all a warm farewell and travelled by taxi the short distance to the small house that Futun bought a few years earlier. Although unhappy, the tenants moved out when they knew that the house would be for the newlyweds and not new tenants.

George and Evelyn never had a honeymoon. Their shortage of funds was compensated, though, by clean air, privacy, and space in their new abode on the hill south of the Old City. They were eager to start married life in Al-Thawri.

5
OUR NEIGHBORHOOD, 1940S

There on the hilltop, Abraham meditated…
faithfulness, the sacrifice of his beloved.
There…evil counsel echoed, thirty pieces
of silver rang hollow…as the Savior expired,
shaking the earth, splitting the rock,
darkening the world, finally resurrecting.
There…bulls and lambs roamed freely

away from bloody knives, from burning
altars. In time, the dirt path winding up
the rocky hill vanished, and so was the fate of
the "weird-looking solitary tree" seen from miles
around. With nature's hand twisted, human
hands molded cement and metal into striking faces,
sharp eyes piercing space, but no ears listened.

Al-Thawri, commonly known as Deir Abu Tor (Monastery of Abu Tor), Abu Tor, or Tori, was rich in nature when George and Evelyn arrived there in 1942. That was most pleasing to them, especially George, who was a consummate gardener.

A pristine, beautiful landscape welcomed the good-looking, young couple. The small, rocky hill opposite their modest house and the open field below their garden were decorated with crown anemone, cyclamen, and honeysuckle. Their garden contained a variety of trees—lemon, olive, and pomegranate—in addition to red geraniums, blue hydrangea, and white jasmine. Their neighbor's garden to the right had one fig tree and several cypress trees. Other neighbors had Jerusalem pine trees. Chamomile, daffodils, yellow daisy, and purple thistle found home in nooks and crannies along their path.

What's in the History, in the Name?

As young Jerusalemites, George and Evelyn were aware of the deep history and powerful religious roots that Jerusalem embodied. Even though Al-Thawri is an integral part of the city, they did not anticipate how their own neighborhood, just a stone's throw away, is equally ancient and timeless and how heavily laden it is with past connections and passion.

Over time, George and Evelyn learned not only that Al-Thawri literally means "the father of the bull," or "father of the ox," but also that the mystery of its bygone days went back further than the bull's story. They increasingly cherished their life in Al-Thawri and made it their home for over seven decades.

Al-Thawri, or the hill to the south of the Old City—which for millennia might have appeared desolate and mysterious to both Jerusalem residents and visitors—is steeped in competing narratives, in addition to historical transformations. There is a possible Paleolithic link, as close-by excavations discovered sizable quantities of flint tools dating to some 300,000 years ago.[101] There is also a probable Canaanite link, as evidenced by rock protrusions forming what looks like an altar that dates back to some 3000-4000 years ago.[102] The Canaanite association is likely, as Jerusalem was originally founded by the Jebusites, an offshoot of the Canaanites.

Moving forward to around 1800 BCE, the Jewish tradition holds that when God tested Abraham by asking him to go to the land of Moriah and offer his beloved son "as a burnt offering on one of the mountains that I shall show you" (Genesis 22:2), he paused on the hill. "There Abraham learned that human sacrifice is not essential to devotion; humans can express fidelity to belief through a symbolic, substitutive act."[103] There, he discovered God's gifts of grace, life, and love. There, each of us can learn to appreciate the deeper truths or mystery of life.

Over the years, Jews have called the hill's upper part by its Arabic name: Abu Tor. In more recent times, and in an effort to Hebraize the names of Jerusalem sites and streets, the Jerusalem Municipality has changed its official name to Givat Hananya (Hananya's Hill), the home location of Hananya or Ananias ben Nebedeus, who officiated as high priest at the end of the Second Temple period, specifically 47 to 52 CE. Josephus Falvius, the 1st century CE Jewish historian, wrote that Hananya's burial ground and monument were on this hill. Josephus also noted that the Roman general, Pompey the Great, set up his camp on this hill when he laid a three-month siege to Jerusalem before it fell in 63 B.C.[104]

The Christian tradition gives importance to the hilltop, both good and bad.[105] The hill is where the Magi or Three Wise Men first saw the star that guided them to Jesus's birthplace in Bethlehem. It designates the general area of the residencies of Joseph Caiaphas, the Jewish high priest who plotted against and participated in the Sanhedrin trial of Jesus. That is why the area is referred to as "the Hill of Evil Counsel." It is where Judas Iscariot—one of the twelve original disciples, who kissed and betrayed Jesus to the Sanhedrin for thirty pieces of silver—hanged himself.[106] It is where a monastery dedicated to St. Luke the Evangelist may have stood. St. Luke is often portrayed with a bull or ox, usually having wings. Was Luke the original Al-Thawri? It is where St. Procopius prayed and where his bones are interred. One can also see the ruins of the Byzantine Church built by Patriarch Modestos II of Jerusalem in the 7th century. Today, the Church of St. Modestos tops the hill within the walls of the Greek Orthodox Compound.

The Arab Muslim tradition has it that Al-Thawri is named after Abu al-ᶜAbas Ahmad ibn Jamal ad-Din ᶜAbdallah ibn Muhammad ibn ᶜAbd al-Jabar al-Qudsi, who inhabited this hill. He was known as "Al-Thawri" because he rode a bull as he witnessed the capture of Jerusalem at the hands of Umar ibn al-Khattab, the second Rightly-Guided Caliph, in April, 637 CE. The bull was actually his messenger. Whenever "Al-Thawri" was unable to go shopping, he would attach the list of goods he needed to the bull's neck, and the bull would go by itself to the city and make the shopping rounds.

Others attribute the name to Ahmed bin Jamal ed-Din, Sheikh Shehab ed-Din el-Qudsi, or Sheikh Ahmed et Toreh, who rode a bull as he fought alongside Salah ed-Din Yusuf ibn Ayyub or Saladin, who captured Jerusalem from the Crusaders in October 1187. His reward: the hillside to the south of the Old City. Whichever story one follows, some believe that Al-Thawri is buried on the hilltop. He rests "in the shadows of a broad fig tree...."[107]

Throughout the centuries, the hill won the attention of special kinds of people: contemplative, prayerful, watchful. Ascetics lived in silence and meditated in its caves. Some were even buried there. Pilgrims climbed its face and fulfilled vows made in foreign lands. They made pledges in its open air. Shepherds tended to their herds, sat under its bushes and trees to escape the hot sun, and contemplated the evening stars.

When the British artist, William Henry Bartlett, visited Jerusalem in 1842, he described the Hill of Evil Counsel as "a bold height, exactly opposite to Zion, and equally rocky and precipitous. From its summit we obtain many important points in the topography of the city." In one steel engraving in which he illustrated Mount Zion from Al-Thawri, one can see two shepherds on a rocky hill tending to a few animals, while six people walk separately in the Hinnom Valley below.[108] In another engraving, there are three Arab shepherds with two animals on a rocky terrain in the foreground, and a fourth shepherd with a large flock at a distance.

Similarly, when Charles William Wilson—an English military officer and one of the foremost pioneer explorers of Jerusalem—first visited Jerusalem in 1864, and intermittently thereafter, he did not see on the hill any housing or farming. Between 1880 and 1884, he published a multi-volume work titled, *Picturesque Palestine*, in which he illustrated in one wood engraving the rocky hill from the south corner of the Old City wall as barren with a lone tree and a walled enclosure atop of it, probably the Greek Orthodox Compound. In contrast, he illustrated the nearer hill-side, part of the ancient City of David, as a good example of terrace cultivation.[109] In another wood engraving, he showed the hill summit with a "weird-looking solitary tree [that] is a landmark for miles around."[110]

In the late 1880s, with the support of a German banker, the Jerusalem businessman, Yosef Navon,[111] and a partner, built two blocks of affordable one-story housing units on the upper-middle, eastern side of the hill, which they called Beit Yosef. A dozen Jewish families moved in. Other Jews lived alongside Arab families elsewhere in the neighborhood. When violence erupted between Arab Muslims and Jews in August 1929—in dispute over access to the Western Wall, causing hundreds of deaths and injury on both sides—conditions for the Jews in Beit Yosef became tense. While the Arab inhabitants of Al-Thawri tried to protect them, they moved away.[112] In the 1930s, a building boom "brought more Jerusalem families to the area as well as British Mandate officials."

It took Jerusalemites several decades to transform Al-Thawri into a habitable locale. When George and Evelyn moved there, there were some houses, but no congestion. Any major construction in Al-Thawri did not begin until the latter part of the 19th century. Arab families—encouraged by the increased security of areas outside the Old City walls and escaping the congestion within the Old City walls—looked for cheap, clean environments, and the hill south of the Old City was one. "[A] number of elite Jerusalem families who were imams, teachers, merchants, and officials…began to settle here, building large spacious homes on the upper part of the hill. These included members of the al-ᶜOouri, Dajani, and Barakat families."[113]

The Vicinity

The road where George and Evelyn moved was without a name, or at least without a name known in the neighborhood, even though the house deed clearly stated it as "El-Kubanieh"—perhaps best translated as "the colony." It resembled, and still resembles, an open-air corridor, with the northern opening facing "Jabal Sahyoun" or "Jabal al-Nabi Dawood" (Mount Zion) and the southern opening facing Wadi Yasul (Valley of Azel) and Jabal al-Mukabbir (Magnifying Mount) above it.

Mount Zion is home to what some believe to be King David's Tomb, Room of the Last Supper, and Dormition Abbey, among other sites. It also has several Christian cemeteries, including Greek Orthodox, Catholic, and Protestant.

Separating El-Kubanieh Road from Mount Zion is the Valley of Hinnom, Gehenna, or Wadi Rababeh (Valley of the Lute), as Palestinians call it. It is the valley of the afflicted, of skulls—where parents believing in different Ba'als and gods during the Canaanite era, like Moloch, "burnt incense" and burnt their "children in the fire" (2 Chronicles 28:3). Some Jews think of Gehenna as the purification stage on the way to the next world. The New Testament speaks of Gehenna as the opposite place to everlasting life. As Matthew 10:28 states, "… rather fear Him who is able to destroy both soul and body in Gehenna." The Qur'an refers to Gehenna as Jahannam, which signifies the final stop of those who reject God, His laws, and His messengers.

Wadi Yasul, or Valley of Azel, is indicated in Zechariah 14:5: "And ye shall flee to the valley of the mountains; for the valley of the mountains shall reach unto Azal: yea, ye shall flee, like as ye fled from before the earthquake in the days of Uzziah king of Judah."

Jabal al-Mukabbir is where Arabs believe that Caliph Umar, approaching Jerusalem with the Muslim forces from the south, stood and declared in a loud voice: "*Allahu Akbar* (God is greatest). This is *Aelia*.[114] We have arrived." It is where the offices of the British High Commissioner were located during the Mandate Period, as well as the Government House, the headquarters of the United Nations Truce Supervisory Organization, since 1948. In between the streets of Al-Thawri and Jabal al-Mukabbir were barren and wooded lands of pine and olive trees.

As for the other two directions, Al-Thawri is bound by Silwan on the East and the German Colony on the West. Silwan, a largely Arab Palestinian neighborhood, was initially built on the eastern slope of the Kidron Valley, but is now on both its sides and extends further to the eastern part of Jabal al-Mukabbir. It is rich in Biblical connections and the site of the Gihon Spring or the Fountain of the Virgin, which is the water source for the Pool of Silwan. The land is fertile, and the inhabitants have made full use of it by earning a living growing and selling vegetables and fruits.

The German Colony was built in the latter part of the 19th century by German Protestants. They belonged to the Temple Society, part of the Pietist Movement of the Lutheran Church, which promoted Messianic salvation in the Holy Land. Their homes resemble the ones they left in Germany, with slanted tiled roofs and shuttered windows, and their livelihoods depended on agriculture and vocational trades, including blacksmithing and carpentry.

Dwelling in Al-Thawri

George and Evelyn did not choose to live in Al-Thawri. They did not choose to live in the house on El-Kubanieh Road; rather it was gifted to them by their "grandmother," Miriam, and "mother/aunt," Futun. They were both fortunate and appreciative, as George's salary was too meager to enable renting or buying an apartment or house.

George and Evelyn's house was located in the set of two row houses that lined the El-Kubanieh Road and the street above it. The main entrance to each house is on the west side and a plot of land is on the east side.[115]

The houses were constructed well, with meter-thick walls that preserved coolness in summer and warmth in winter, high ceilings, domed roofs, and Armenian tiled floors. The houses also had arched windows that gave way to verandas, courtyards, and, in some instances, gardens of "the seven fruits of the Bible." The cobblestone, cement, or tile, creating a path along the front of each house was smoothed by the footsteps of time.

George and Evelyn's house had a domed roof, as did their neighbor's house on the left. The neighbor's house on the right had one of the few red terracotta roofs. Most other houses had flat roofs. George and Evelyn could look at the panoramic view from their garden after rainfall and see the sky reflected in them. Water tanks were added a few years later, followed decades later by television antennae and satellite dishes.

As George and Evelyn walked El-Kubanieh and its adjacent streets, they met many of their neighbors. All were welcoming. Among them were Christian families, including Al-Aʿraj, Munayyer, Simonian, and Sruji, who had lived there from before the 1940s and 1930s. All the others in El-Kubanieh, and actually in the entire neighborhood, were, and are, Muslim Arab families. Among them are Abu ʿAsab, ʿAtieh, Barakat, Jadaʿ, Salhab, Siam, and Zuʿaiter. Families like Abu ʿAsab and Salhab originated from al-Khalil (Hebron), a city located some 28km to the southwest of Jerusalem.[116] They came in search of work and stayed. Their migration from the rural to the urban areas of Palestine was mostly due to the "economic instability predicated in part on changes in the agricultural realm."[117]

George and Evelyn's next-door neighbor, Mariam or Umm Yousef, originally from Lebanon, was gracious. She often acted as their resource person. She moved out a couple years later after selling her house.

Even though Al-Thawri was a short walking distance from the Old City, the area where George and Evelyn lived lacked several basic amenities, including running water, sewerage, and electricity. Municipal services were nonexistent. This was far different from what they were used to at the Swedish School, where these amenities and services existed and were taken for granted. Like pioneers, they had to be creative and do with little to survive. It took commitment, courage, and resilience not to give up.

What helped George and Evelyn was a well in the field below their garden, which the neighbors tapped for drinking water. Qadrieh, a female neighbor in the street above, would fetch water for them and was paid per gallon. Water for bathing and toilet use was transported in large rubber jugs by donkey from the ancient Silwan Pool. The sewerage issue was resolved by constructing a simplified waste disposal system beneath the garden. Kerosene lamps and candles provided the light, while kerosene heaters provided much needed warmth in the winter. *Fallahaat* (female farmers or peasants) from Silwan roamed the streets during morning hours to sell fruits and vegetables. Raya sold milk; her family had a couple of cows. Staple food and household items had to be secured in the Old City.

George and Evelyn also enjoyed exploring neighborhoods beyond their own. Among these were Baqʿa, Talbiya, German Colony, Greek Colony, and, of course, Katamon—where Evelyn's father, Jani, lived.

Once Evelyn got married, relations between her and her father improved significantly. Her father welcomed George and always treated him with deference. George reciprocated with pleasure. Evelyn visited her father and stepmother, Louisa, on a regular basis. She played with her younger stepsisters, Loreh, Leila, and Nadira and younger stepbrothers, George, Dimitri, and Alexander. She grew close to them.

Raising a Family, Our Family

George's work at the Greek Orthodox Patriarchal Press was only part-time, and his monthly salary was totally inadequate to support a family. The inflation that accompanied the Second World War in Palestine put those on fixed income in dire straits. Writing about that period's economic situation, Wasif Jawhariyyeh contrasts the prices before and during the war: 3 kilograms of olive oil jumped from 10 to 110 piasters; a canister of ghee from 120 piasters to 18 pounds; a sack of premium quality flour from 96 piasters to 9 pounds; a bottle of Johnny Walker whiskey from 40 piasters to 4 pounds; and a prêt-a-porter fine-wool suit from 5 to 25 pounds.[118] Similarly, Sami ʿAmr titled his diary, dated March 10, 1942, "Famine Threatens Us from One Day to the Next!!" and bemoaned the high prices of staples or their lack thereof.[119]

With the blessings of Father Modestos, his boss at the printing press, and Evelyn's encouragement, George applied and started work at the Government Printing Press, located a five-minute walk from the house. That saved George travel time to and from the Old City, gave him a higher salary, and opened new opportunities for him. Typeset publications at the Government Printing Press were secular, focusing on economic and political reports and the issuing of *Palestinian Facts*. The work environment there was diverse.

Unlike the Greek Orthodox Patriarchal Printing Press, where all the workers were Christian, his co-workers at the Government Printing Press included Jews and Muslims as well. Ishaq (Isaac) Klein, a co-worker and a good friend, lived in the Old City's Jewish Quarter and spoke Arabic fluently. When conditions worsened in Jerusalem, my father advised him to relocate from the Jewish Quarter to Musherem (Mea Shearim), a Jewish neighborhood outside the walled city, but Ishaq loved where he lived. Tragically, he was killed one day close to his home. It was a great loss, felt deeply by all his co-workers. The assailant was never caught.

George and Evelyn began to think seriously about starting a large family. Not yet seventeen, Evelyn gave birth to a baby girl, my oldest sister, at the government maternity hospital in the Russian Compound. Mariam, our maternal great grandmother, and Futun, our mother's aunt, but more so our grandmother, were present to lend a hand. George rushed from work to be there, and all three then accompanied our mother and sister back to Al-Thawri. Our sister was named Fatina, Arabic for captivating, which is related to Futun. Derivative of the Greek word or name Photini, it means light or the enlightened one. Perhaps beauty is accentuated by brightness.

Relatives and neighbors, carrying baklava, chocolates, and baby clothes, came in droves that late summer of 1943 to extend their congratulations, as did grandfather Jani and his family. To everyone's delight, Tatiana, our father's caretaker, visited as well. Our mother remembered the visit as if it were yesterday. "Wearing a crème knee-length dress and a matching head scarf with tiny flowers, Tatiana sat with us under the large lemon tree. Placing Fatina on her lap, she cried, saying: 'Vanya's (that is, Ivan's, later changed to George) parents would have been ecstatic to see their granddaughter.' Pointing her right index finger upwards, she added, 'I know they are.'" That was the last time they heard or saw Tatiana. It is as if she had fulfilled her promise. It is as if all was fine with the heavens![120]

Our mother became pregnant again. Tragically, our great-grandmother passed away that same year, which was devastating to everyone, particularly grandmother Futun and her sister, Julia, and our mother. Mariam, as matriarch, held the family together for years, and it was she, with everyone's help, who cared for our mother when her mother or our maternal grandmother, Anastasia, died. Mariam was buried at the Greek Orthodox Cemetery in the same tomb as her daughter.

Our mother was carrying twins, but had a miscarriage, which would be devastating to any mother, let alone a very young mother. What was more devastating was the diagnosis of her gynecologist: "You can't get pregnant again." A second medical opinion proved otherwise. With proper medication, our mother gave birth to our second sister. That was great news, as it gave our mother reassurance about her ability to carry a pregnancy to full term.

Our second sister was named Anastas, or Anastasia, after our maternal grandmother. Anastasia is related to Anastasis, which means resurrection in Greek, usually the Resurrection of Jesus. But the name also pleased our father; Anastasia was Czar Nicholas and Czarina Alexandra's youngest daughter.

A year later, our mother again became pregnant with twins. As before, she had a miscarriage and deeply felt the loss. Questions increased as to why the miscarriages were happening. Was it something our mother was doing or not doing? Our mother did not drink or smoke or swear! To our mother's best knowledge, there were no abnormalities, disorders, or untreated illnesses....

In 1947, our mother gave birth to our eldest brother, Khamis. Without knowing the baby's gender yet, when our father was asked by his co-workers at the Government Printing Press, he responded, "a girl." They teased him, calling him *abu al-banat*, meaning father of the girls. While our parents never minded the gender of their newborn, for they considered every baby to be "a gift from God," the preference in the Middle East, particularly Arab society, was and still is for boys.[121] When our father's co-workers heard it was a boy, they insisted on sweets. The next day, our father expended half his week's salary, bringing baklava to work.

Our oldest brother, Khamis, carries our adoptive paternal grandfather's name. Being the first son, his name attached itself to our parents' names, as is customary in Arab culture, even though our parents retained their names for daily use or formal documentation. Our father, George, became the father of Khamis or Abu Khamis; our mother, Evelyn, became the mother of Khamis or Imm Khamis. Amusingly, the name Khamis means Thursday, while Khamis was born on a Monday!

Following the death of her mother, George's increased salary at the Government Printing Press, and George and Evelyn's growing family, Futun realized that it was the right time for her to leave her housekeeper position at the Swedish School, which she did. She moved in with George and Evelyn—into the same house she bought in 1937—lived in the same large bedroom as everyone else, and devoted the rest of her life to raising their children.

One of her first tasks, however, was to resolve our mother's frequent nightmares. "After arriving in Al-Thawri," our mother described, "I would wake up in the middle of the night screaming. Something was suffocating me. That was both disturbing and frightening." Futun consulted with a couple of trusted neighbors. The diagnosis: the Evil Eye, a malefic spirit or ghoul. The prescription: a pig's nose to be hung at the bedroom's door. The explanation: the pig and its flesh are considered unclean, and there are religious restrictions in the consumption of pork, especially in Islamic (and Jewish) laws. Even the bad spirit would not dare come close to the pig's nose! "My aunt immediately contacted the Siniora family," our mother added, "who owned a pig farm and was well-known in the processed meat industry. A pig's nose was cleaned, salted, and dried. I have not had any screaming episodes ever since." What will my family do, what will people do without their myths and superstitions, without their remedies and solutions? Unfortunately, these do not ward off larger evils and wars, let alone make life easier.

Inevitably, life has its own twists and turns. Our free will is only free to a certain degree. Overnight, whatever is smooth can become rough, and whatever is straight can become twisted. Dreams, more often than not, can turn into nightmares. The small decisions we make can frequently be overruled or sidetracked by larger decisions made by others. Time and again, those who sow the wind force others to reap the whirlwind, and that is what materialized for many innocent people, including the Sarsar family, in the late 1940s.

6
War, 1948

The innocent…were blown up to smithereens. Children, pregnant women, were tortured to death…. Soldiers, civilians looted; they looted homes like mad, for days. Wounded hands in the dust, in mounds of rubble, reach to the sky.

With what right do we kill, dehumanize, dispossess? The offenders' list is long. The vultures feast at the valley of slaughter. The eagles fly in the Heavenly Jerusalem where no wall, no tomb, no rock stands. Life is but a shadow of the bright light. Let's be there.

1948 is imprinted in the hearts and minds of all Israelis and Palestinians, but for different reasons. It is the decisive year when the proclamation of the State of Israel and Israel's War of Independence occurred. It is when the majority of Palestinians who lived in what became Israel lost their homes and sources of revenue, in what they call Al-Nakba or catastrophe. What materialized then, and since, has set in motion successive wars between Israel and its neighbors and brought about fear, bloodshed, insecurity, or destitution to millions.

The British Mandate, established in the early 1920s,[122] was nearing its end in the 1940s. British officials, who basically had fulfilled their mission by enabling the creation of a "national home" for the Jewish people, could no longer manage the daily affairs of Palestine. They asked that what was entrusted to them by the League of Nations be turned over to its successor organization, the United Nations.

The Palestinian Arab and Jewish communities became "disgruntled and antagonized, and each successively rose in rebellion against British rule, which was to terminate amid bloodshed, chaos, recrimination, and ignominy."[123] Their respective leaders played deadly zero-sum games, even though they were of unequal influence and strength at different junctures during the British Mandate. By the early 1940s, and as a direct result of how the British squashed the Arab Revolt, "Palestinian society was economically devastated, politically and militarily defeated, and psychologically crushed."[124] Its preparations could not withstand the Zionist offensive. Jewish society was more viable, politically, financially, and militarily. Its paramilitary groups, both moderate and extremist, were better led and organized[125] than the Palestinian militia and volunteers. As explained by Issa J. Boullata, "the Palestinian leadership was in disarray" and did not put forward well-thought out policies with regard to the British and the United Nations. In contrast, "the Jewish political leadership was organized and had clear-cut goals. Its military activities had strategic aims, were well supplied with weapons…and used all possible tactics to achieve their goals."[126]

Eventually, on November 29, 1947, the United Nations General Assembly passed Resolution 181 (II),[127] with thirty-three votes in favor, thirteen against, and ten abstentions. Calling mainly for partitioning Palestine into an Arab state and a Jewish state, for an economic union between them, and for Jerusalem to be a *corpus separatum*—a separate entity under a special international regime—the resolution was rejected by the Arab states and the Palestinian Arabs, but accepted by the Jews. The Arabs were angry and observed a three-day strike in Jerusalem and the rest of Palestine. The Jews were jubilant and celebrated with dance and songs.

As soon as the British Mandate flag was lowered over Palestine, David Ben-Gurion—the Chair of the Jewish Agency for Palestine and the Executive Head of the World Zionist Organization—proclaimed the State of Israel on May 14, 1948, leading Jews in Tel Aviv, Jerusalem, and beyond toward jubilation, and Palestinians toward anger and mourning. It also pushed Arab forces from Egypt, Syria, Transjordan (later Jordan), Lebanon, and Iraq to invade. The ensuing war gave Israel the opportunity to acquire more territory than what was allocated to it under the Partition Resolution (Map 4). The remaining territory ended up under Jordanian and Egyptian jurisdictions, with the former keeping East Jerusalem and the West Bank, and the latter retaining control of the Gaza Strip.

The Palestinian community was dispossessed, as expressed in Al-Nakba, and the independent Arab state (of Palestine) was nowhere to be seen. Instead, Palestinian refugees were the outcome. Between June 1, 1946 and May 15, 1948, around seven-hundred-fifty-thousand people "lost both home and means of livelihood," and most wound up in refugee camps in Jerusalem, the West Bank, the Gaza Strip, Jordan, Lebanon, and Syria.[128]

The bloody engagements of both sides and the British response to them before and after the passage of UNGA Resolution 181—as well as the 1948 war between Israel and the Arab states—made the lives of ordinary people "hell on earth." People were hesitant to venture out unless it was essential. To control Jerusalem, the British divided it into various security zones, with checkpoints and limited access between them. Acts of terror became common occurrences. The list is long—very long—and its cumulative effects propelled many, including my parents, to leave their homes for safer areas.

Map 4: Comparison of 1947 Partition Plan Borders and Armistice Lines of 1949

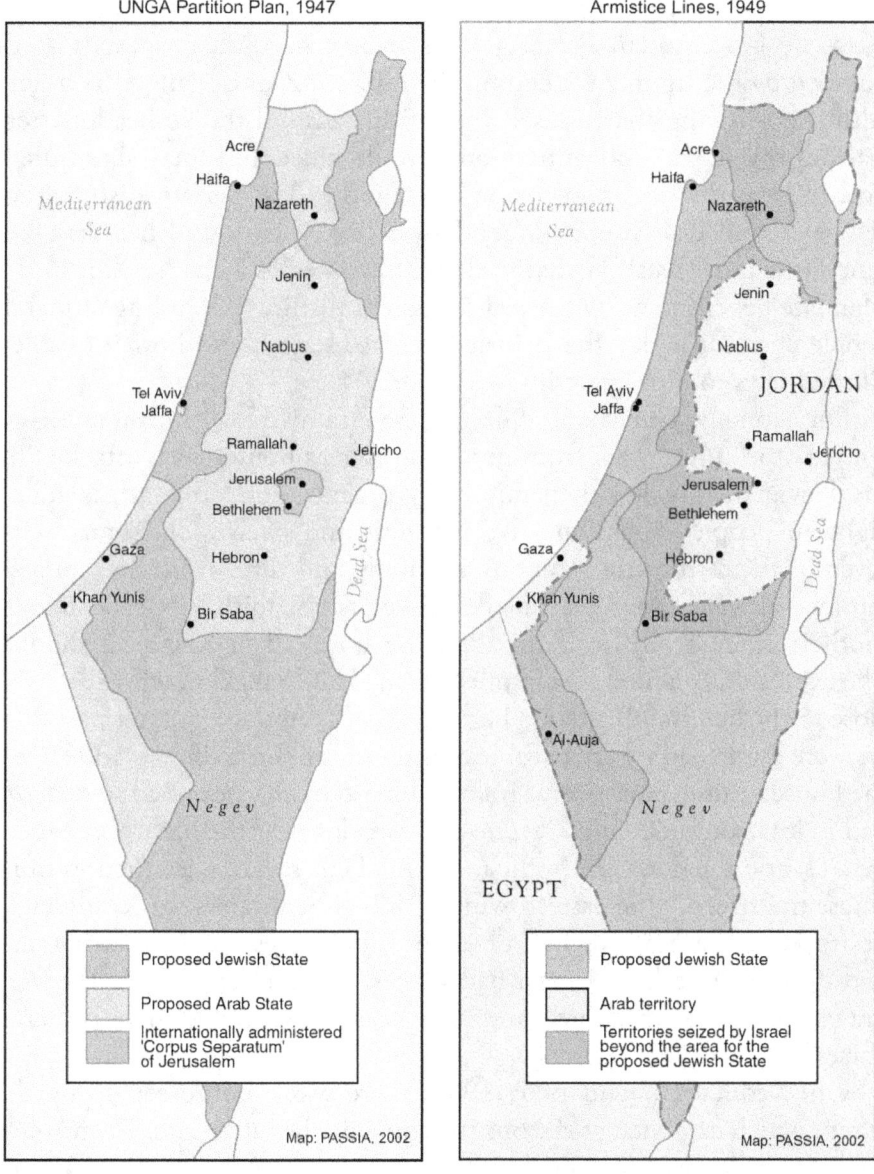

Terror and Heavy Loss

On Monday, July 22, 1946, the King David Hotel—a ten-minute walk from Al-Thawri (where my family lived) and a five-minute walk from the Government Printing Press (where my father worked)—was bombed by the Irgun Zvei Leumi, the militant Zionist gang. The hotel's entire south wing that housed the British administrative headquarters was destroyed. The toll: ninety-one people killed and forty-six injured. To her great disbelief and sorrow, my mother lost her Swedish School classmate and dear friend, Mary Bawarchi. "They found her with her lunch in hand." Wasif Jawhariyyeh, who worked as a civil servant in the Mandate government, witnessed Jerusalem turning into a huge funeral. People cursed the day the British Mandate started and how it enabled allowed Jews to immigrate into Palestine.[129]

On Monday, January 5, 1948, the Semiramis Hotel in Katamon—a couple of minutes' walk from my grandfather's house—was attacked by the Haganah, the Jewish paramilitary organization. This attack killed eighteen people—including five Muslims and twelve Christians, with seven of them from the Abu Suwan family and three from the Lorenzo family—as well as Manuel Allende Salazar, the Spanish Vice-Consul. My mother remembered her father relaying how "all of Katamon shook." The explosion "planted fear in our hearts." Hala Sakakini, who also lived close to the Semiramis, shared her reflections: "About a quarter past one, we were awakened by an awful explosion that lighted the sky and shook the house. This explosion was followed by shots that sounded so near we had to leave our beds and creep to the corridor near the bathroom where we all sat on the floor...." In the morning, Hala saw the destruction from across the street: "The eastern wing of Hotel Semiramis was completely destroyed. It was nothing but a heap of rubble. Despite the pouring rain and bitter cold, a large crowd had gathered at the scene. All faces were drawn and pale with sadness and fury. Women wept, and men muttered curses."[130]

On Wednesday, January 7, 1948, there was a bomb set up by the Irgun, which exploded at the bus stop outside the Jaffa Gate. Twenty-five Palestinian Arabs were killed and many injured. Marie Majaj, wife of Najib Majaj and mother of a two-year-old boy and a five-month-old girl, was killed. Najib, the cousin of Dr. Amin Majaj, our pediatrician, was injured.[131] Issa Boullata was passing by and "miraculously escaped from dying…."[132]

On Sunday, February 1, 1948, an attack was carried out against the *Palestine Post*—a Jewish-owned newspaper—by Khalil Janho, a member of the Palestinian Arab irregulars and a worker at the Central Prison. Disguised as a British policeman and driving a military-style truck carrying the explosives, he passed the checkpoint and penetrated the Jewish restricted zone off Jaffa Road.[133] The enormous explosion killed at least three civilians and injured thirty.

On Sunday, February 22, 1948, one Palestinian Arab man and two British deserters, dressed in British uniforms, drove an armored car and two truck bombs onto Ben Yehuda Street in Jerusalem. The explosions destroyed four buildings, resulting in the deaths of fifty-seven Jewish civilians and wounding dozens. Meron Benvenisti—former deputy mayor of Jerusalem who lived in our neighborhood of Al-Thawri for a while—remembers how, at age fourteen, he assisted in clearing the rubble: "The English offered earth-moving equipment, on condition that they themselves operate it, but the Jewish Agency refused, so that's how they brought us in to do the work. I remember that I bent down to clear something and suddenly I saw a human hand sticking out of the rubble. This is a sight that I will of course never forget."[134]

On Thursday, March 11, 1948, there was a major attack on the heavily guarded offices of the Jewish Agency for Palestine, which housed the Jewish paramilitary organization, Haganah, and other Jewish national institutions. Anton Da'ud Kamilyo, the Armenian American driver of the U.S. Consul General, drove the green Ford limousine into the compound and left it there with 220 pounds of TNT in its trunk. A guard rolled the car away but it exploded, killing thirteen Jews—including the chair of the Jewish National Fund—and injuring some one-hundred people, in addition to partial destruction of the structure.[135]

On Friday, April 9, 1948, members of the Irgun and the Stern Gang militia, known as Lehi, attacked the 750 villagers of Deir Yassin, located between Jerusalem and Tel Aviv. At least one-hundred-seven of them were murdered, many of them in cold blood. This massacre coincided with the funeral of Abd al-Qader al-Husseini, the Palestinian Arab commander of al-Jihad al-Muqaddas (Holy War Army)—volunteers who died on April 8 fighting the Jewish forces in the key Battle for Al-Qastal. Fifty-five orphans of Deir Yassin, found near the Church of Holy Sepulchre, were cared for by Hind al-Husseini, the cousin of Abd al-Qader.[136] She converted her grandfather's house into an orphanage, Dar al-Tifl al-Arabi (Home of the Arab Child).

On Wednesday, April 14, 1948, a Jewish medical convoy was ambushed by Palestinian Arab forces in Sheikh Jarrah on its way to Hadassah Hospital on Mount Scopus: "The British Army, though fully aware of the ensuing battle, waited six hours before intervening. By then seventy-six Jews, including forty medical staff, had been killed, some as they tried to escape the burning vehicles. A British soldier and 14 Arabs were also shot dead."[137]

Displacement and Dispossession

In 1947-1948, nearly all the Palestinian Arab residents of West Jerusalem fled or were expelled from their neighborhoods in Lifta, Ein Karim, Deir Yassin, El-Maliha, Katamon, Greek Colony, German Colony, Baqʿa, Talbiyeh, Abu Tor, Mamillah, and Musrara, among others. Out of despair, fear, and or threats, they left for the eastern parts of Jerusalem and beyond, hoping to return to their houses when the violence stopped. In his diaries about the 1948 war in the Old City, Constantine X. Mavrides—Liaison Land Representative of the R.G. Consulate of Greece, and a future relative—[138] wrote of their plight and the support they received thereafter:

> "Long before May 14, many inhabitants of the Muslim and Christian suburbs of the city—those who had not gone abroad—took refuge in the Old City... People took refuge in the houses of relatives and friends... convents, monasteries, and patriarchates willingly received members from their congregations, as well as other members from different congregations, and offered them shelter."[139]

The family of Jacob J. Nammar decided not to leave their home in Haret al-Nammareh, a residential area of lower Baqʿa. It was not long before they had to leave home against their wishes and become confined to "Prison Zone A."[140] The Nammar Family was never allowed to return home.

Tawfiq and Mary Bayyouk, my wife's maternal grandparents, left their house near Musrara "only with the clothes on their backs." After an eighteen-month displacement in Ramallah, they returned to Jerusalem, but their house became located on the Israeli side of the border. With no other residence and with no jobs, they were forced to live in the small tailor shop they rented inside the Old City's New Gate. In search of work, Tawfiq secured a low-paying job as a tailor with the Jordanian army and visited with his family three times a year. Mary later moved in a small apartment provided by the Roman Catholic Church. She cared for her children, working as a seamstress, but barely managing to make both ends meet.

My Greek grandfather, Jani, dispatched his wife, Louisa (our step-grandmother), and six children to Transjordan (which officially changed its name to the Hashemite Kingdom of Jordan in 1949) to escape the violence and be with his paternal aunt, Frosso Damianou Korfiatis, and her husband, Farah Abu Jaber[141] in As-Salt, thirty-five-and-a-half miles (57 km) northeast of Jerusalem. It is there that they spent close to a year, while Jani continued living in Katamon and working in the facilities department at Hansen Hospital (formerly the Jesus Hilfe Hospice) in the Talbiyeh neighborhood. Upon returning to his two-story house one day, he found it occupied by two Jewish families, one on each floor. It took money and weeks of negotiations, with the help of the Greek Consulate, to buy the two families out and reclaim his house. His family used their Greek passports to return to Katamon from Transjordan.

All in all, some 80,000 Palestinian Arabs were forced to move from West Jerusalem. Most of them lost all of their belongings, and their homes and private properties were ransacked. Widespread looting took place. Israel confiscated around 10,000 houses and 13.51358 square miles (35km^2) of land[142] and distributed them among Jewish immigrants and refugees. The unlucky Palestinian Arabs—those unable to find shelter in East Jerusalem and its environs or abroad—ended up in over fifty refugee camps located in the Gaza Strip, West Bank, Syria, Lebanon, and Jordan.[143]

For their part, the 2,500 Jews who lived in the Old City's Jewish Quarter were besieged by Arab forces. Jewish resistance, mainly by the Haganah and the Irgun, inside and outside the quarter, was to no avail.

Those who survived the battle for the Jewish Quarter between May 15 and 18, 1948, were rounded up and later repatriated through the Red Cross to West Jerusalem. Whatever was left of their properties was taken over by the Jordanian Custodian of Enemy Property and distributed to the Palestinian Arab refugees.[144]

Efforts to redress the loss hit a dead end, including United General Assembly Resolution 194 of December 11, 1948, which resolved that:

> "the refugees wishing to return to their homes and live at peace with their neighbors should be permitted to do so at the earliest practicable date, and that compensation should be paid for the property of those choosing not to return and for loss of or damage to property which, under principles of international law or equity, should be made good by the Governments or authorities responsible."[145]

My Family's Flight

In May 1948, my family consisting of my father, mother, grandmother Futun, Fatina (five years), Anastasia (three years), and Khamis (one year), faced the dilemma of staying or leaving. The continuous acts of violence and the bombing, mortar-shelling, and rifle-firing associated with the siege of Jerusalem's Old City were more than enough to tip the balance in favor of fleeing to a safer place. There was no telling how long the sojourn would be or if the house would be destroyed or taken over by others while vacant.

My father rented a truck—an expensive proposition at that time because of fuel shortages caused by damage to installations in Haifa and to the railway and roads[146]—and loaded it with most of the house furniture and supplies. With my grandmother, mother, and baby Khamis in the front cabin, and my father, Fatina, and Anastasia in the back, the truck headed toward Ariha (Jericho), the famed historic city, located fifteen miles (24 km) northeast of Jerusalem, near the Jordan River and Dead Sea. The roads were jammed with people and traffic—all heading in the same direction: toward supposed safety.

My grandmother's brother-in-law's brother, Tawfiq Nasser Mukhar, owned the large Bellevue Hotel in Jericho and welcomed them to "the organized madness." They rented a couple of rooms, one for my parents and baby Khamis, and another for my grandmother and sisters, Fatina and Anastasia. There was no extra storage space for furniture.

Leaving my grandmother and my three siblings at the hotel, my parents proceeded to cross the Jordan River to reach Suwaylih, twenty-five miles (40 km) northeast of Jericho. That's where Julia (Futun's sister) and Nicola Nasser Mukhar and their children lived after fleeing Musrara a couple months earlier, and that is where they left the furnishings for safekeeping.

Returning to the Bellevue, my parents could not believe the stressed environment around them. The city was teaming with people and bundles from all over Palestine. People were lost, trying to figure out their next move and loaf of bread. People were angry at having to leave their homes, lives, and livelihoods behind. Wasif Jawhariyyeh, who experienced Jericho in 1948, and who also stayed at the Bellevue Hotel in 1949, reflected on the tragedy that befell Palestinians: "[E]veryone seemed as though they were at a funeral, thinking about what they had become overnight, cursing the British, the Jewish settlers, the Arabs, the states, and the armies, and crying over the destiny and the future of their children who had lost their country and were without shelter."[147]

While at the Bellevue Hotel, my mother faced hell and almost died. She got increasingly sick, with a high fever. The physician consulted diagnosed an infection, but was uncertain about the culprit. It reached a point where my mother's mouth was so inflamed that she could not open it or swallow anything. That, in turn, interfered with her breathing and her food intake. She had to use a straw to drink some tea and chamomile.

Alerted to this medical emergency, Mr. Mukhar, the hotel owner—highly respected and connected in Jericho—brought an army medical doctor to the hotel. Speaking with a Lebanese accent, the doctor (probably a graduate of the School of Medicine at the American University of Beirut) gave a quick diagnosis in two simple words: "min drasha" (from her teeth). He contacted a dentist friend, Dr. Adamany, who promptly put my mother on a penicillin regimen. This antibiotic was just being introduced in Palestine, and each unit was extremely expensive. My mother had to sell two of her four 22k gold bracelets to pay the resultant medical costs.

When my mother broke her teeth in secondary school, the dentist in Ramallah supposedly filled her back teeth with gold. An examination by Dr. Adamany revealed instead an amalgam filling, mainly consisting of mercury, silver, and copper. Aside from the thievery and criminal act by the dentist, the filling must have been defective or become damaged over time, and my mother was suffering from severe amalgam poisoning. Mercury and mercury vapor are toxic, and exposure can lead to gum inflammation and kidney damage. Mercury poisoning in women especially can impede pregnancy or result in miscarriages. Excessive levels of copper can cause anemia and hurt the liver, kidney, and immune system.

A male staff nurse with the Arab Legion (later Jordanian army), George Haddad, known as Abu Emil, showed up at the hotel numerous times over several days to give my mother penicillin shots. The inflamed gums and dental abscess had to be reduced before any dental work could be started. Regrettably, Dr. Adamany saw no way of salvaging my mother's teeth; they were far gone and filled with puss. The decision was made to operate. If the pain from inflammation and fever was excruciating, it became magnified a hundredfold when the teeth extraction was done without anesthesia: "The pain was far worse than labor pain," my mother commented. As each tooth was being pulled out, puss oozed and oozed. A few weeks later, my mother began wearing dentures at age twenty-two.

The stay at the Bellevue lasted from May through November. Even though the war was ongoing, my father travelled by bus from Jericho to Damascus Gate bus station in Jerusalem and back once a month to ensure that the house in Al-Thawri was secure. As the fighting began to subside in Jerusalem, my family left Jericho and headed first to ⁽Atara, a village to the north of Ramallah. There, they rented a single room for a few months before returning home.

By then, the fighting was over and the post-war fate of Jerusalem was being decided. Two commanding officers were charged with drawing up a new map indicating temporary borders so as to keep the peace: the Israeli Lt. Col. Moshe Dayan and the Jordanian Lt. Col. Abdullah El-Tell. With a large map laid on an unsmooth surface in a deserted Jerusalem house on Tuesday, November 30, 1948, the two officers carved up the city:

"Dayan used a red grease pencil. [El-]Tell used a green one. Their lines rarely met. For the men, the lines were drawn only to reflect the general position of their forces on the front lines.... The two men didn't expect their rough work to mark the final, firm border."[148]

The areas between the red and green lines became no man's land, and one such area bordered our neighborhood. On the west side of it developed the Israeli section of Abu Tor, and on the east side of it developed the Arab Jordanian section of Al-Thawri.

The other Palestinian Arab neighborhoods in West Jerusalem, including Katamon, German Colony, Baqʿa, Talbiya, and Musrara, became the home of Jewish immigrants from Eastern Europe and the Middle East. Israeli leaders, such as Moshe Dayan, wanted to create a *fait accompli*. As Arnon Golan explained, "The population by Jews of former Arab neighborhoods was supposed to create facts on the ground, after which it would be difficult to alter them in the framework of a political agreement."[149] Creating such facts on the Israeli side generated internal disagreements over the allocation of the Palestinian Arab houses to Jews."[150]

The 1948 War—called the First Arab-Israeli War—resulted in other major developments that dictated the future of Jerusalem and the rest of the Arab-Israeli region for years, such as joining of the West Bank with the East Bank of the Jordan, and placing the Gaza Strip under Egyptian control.[151] An armistice agreement was reached between Israel and each of its surrounding Arab states of Egypt, Lebanon, Syria, and Jordan. The Israel-Jordan Armistice Agreement was signed at Rhodes on April 3, 1949, under auspices of the United Nations.

In the meantime, my mother became pregnant after returning home and gave birth in 1949 to my second oldest brother, this time at the Austrian Hospice across from the Third Station of Via Dolorosa (Way of Sorrows). Choosing his name has a story. My mother explained, "A tall young man in a white robe appeared to me in a dream before giving birth. He said that I will have a son and commanded that I name him Mikhaeel." She believed it was Archangel Michael, the head of all angels and the supreme commander of God's army. A dilemma arose, as the birth was happening in early August on the feast of the Prophet Elijah, or Mar Elias. Abu Emil, the Arab Legion officer (who gave my mother the penicillin injections) was transferred to Al-Thawri and brought his family with him to visit my family that week. Upon learning of this predicament, he split a piece of plain paper in two and wrote "Michel" on the first and "Elias" on the second. He called my four-year old sister, Anastasia, over and asked her to pick one of them. "Michel" it was, and that's how Michel's name came to be. Without the dream, the archangel's command, and the officer's wisdom, Michel might have been named Elias.

The internal displacement and waiting in Jericho and ᶜAtara were intensely painful. Returning home was not easy. It seems that wars do not end when the shooting stops. Conditions became precarious and more difficult in between and surrounding the red and green lines in Al-Thawri. But, life went on, as it must.

7
OUR NEIGHBORHOOD, 1950-2000

Our neighborhoods become
healthier when we protect them,
when we feel protected in them.
Our houses transform into homes
when we belong, when we let love in,
indifference out. Our games turn
enjoyable, more meaningful, when

we fight to share with others, not
win over them. Our words carry
weight when we empower others,
when we earn their respect.
"Stop dreaming," you might say.
"Without dreams," I say,
"tomorrow remains in the past."

The separation between East Jerusalem and West Jerusalem was immediate. It had a lasting impact on my family and all Jerusalemites. Jordanian soldiers faced Israeli soldiers across no man's land.

Jerusalem became a powder keg. "Problems along the border only got worse as the years dragged on with no agreement on what to do… Snipers from both sides kept shooting. Civilians kept dying. The United Nations kept holding emergency meetings to contain the violence."[152] Those daring to confront no man's land took their lives into their own hands. In July 1954 alone, sniper fire killed nine people and injured fifty-five along the border in Jerusalem.[153]

Given its key position along the Old City-southern Jerusalem line, "Abu Tor [/Al-Thawri] became a problematic focal point of armistice violations where several military positions were located right in the midst of the civilian population of both parties…."[154] Some Al-Thawri families whose houses abutted or were within no man's land abandoned them and moved to houses nearby. This tense condition, in one form or another, lasted from 1949 to 1967.

Another major challenge during the same period related to a wider conflict or competition between the Palestinians and the Jordanian leadership, as Jordan became the ruling authority over East Jerusalem and the West Bank. Consequentially, "the Palestinian political decision and national entity disappeared, and the Palestinians were deprived of their right to exercise their self-determination…."[155]

The secret talks King Abdullah held with Israeli leaders over the Jerusalem Question and other issues angered some Palestinians. Mustapha Shukri Ashu, a twenty-one-year-old tailor apprentice from Jerusalem, assassinated the king at the Al-Aqsa Mosque on July 20, 1951, which resulted in the wrath of the Arab Legion in East Jerusalem and a wave of arrests. More than thirty Palestinian Arabs were killed, and many were wounded. Ten conspirators were named—including the ex-Military Governor of Jerusalem Colonel Abdullah El-Tell and Dr. Musa Abdullah al-Husseini, a cousin of ex-Mufti of Jerusalem Hajj Amin el-Husseini—but only six were found guilty and sentenced to death.[156]

Jerusalem, in official Jordanian eyes, was secondary to the capital, Amman, from where the administrative, economic, and political life emanated, and where the influence and power of the state apparatus were centralized. Several government offices were relocated from Jerusalem to the capital, the request to create an Arab university in East Jerusalem was rejected, and economic revitalization projects were rare. Socialists and communists were hunted down and imprisoned. "The monarchy pursued a policy of political fragmentation buttressed by economic backwardness that aimed to prevent the formation of large political parties or newly wealthy groups independent of its control who might challenge Husayn's rule."[157] The Hashemite strategy towards the Palestinians was "essentially one of cooptation mixed with repression."[158]

Occasional anti-government riots in Jerusalem took place—in 1951, 1955, 1956, 1957, and 1963—and were dealt with harshly. The riots were caused, in part, by the opposition to the Hashemite King, the resurgence of Palestinian nationalism, and the rise of pan-Arabism and Nasserism. Palestinian nationalism began to reassert itself after it had been sidetracked, mostly by Israel, Jordan, and Egypt, which absorbed the Arab state promised in the UN General Assembly Resolution 181 (II). Gamal Abdel-Nasser, Egypt's president, won the hearts and minds of the Arab masses with his vision of Arab socialism and Arab unity. Many Palestinians found strength in his backing of the Palestinian Liberation Organization. I heard stories of how soldiers would stop and interrogate students, asking them if they were *talamiz*, meaning pupils, or *tullab*, meaning seekers of knowledge.[159] The latter response resulted in a beating, or potentially even worse treatment, because the soldiers interpreted it as favoring revolution.

In contrast, there were those who appreciated the Jordanian presence in Jerusalem, as it brought a modicum of security, stability, and prosperity. Among them were prominent families, like the Nashashibis and Nusseibehs, who were cultivated by the kingdom and occupied important posts in the government. The East Jerusalem-Jericho-Amman road (72 kilometers or 44.7 miles) was widened, enabling better access between the East and West banks of the Jordan River. Kalandia Airport, located between Jerusalem and Ramallah, was opened, the Intercontinental Hotel was built atop the Mount of Olives, and tourists flowed into the holy sites. Families living on both sides of the Jordan had no problems visiting each other, as we and the Mukhar family in Amman did on many occasions.

Coping with Change

My family, like all others, did its best to manage, but it was difficult. The division of Jerusalem between East and West blocked the easy access from Al-Thawri to the Old City via Jaffa Gate or New Gate, which usually took fifteen minutes to reach. Our family had to travel through the Silwan and Kidron Valleys, in order to reach East Jerusalem—a trip that often necessitated waiting for the bus to leave the main station, or arriving at the local stops in addition to the half hour for the trip itself. Travel costs increased as well. When we were short on cash, or the buses were unavailable, we took what we called "Bus # 11," meaning we walked through the Valley of Hinnom or Wadi al-Rababeh (Valley of the Lute) along the side of a water pipe, hence the Way of the Pipe, in order to enter the Old City from Dung Gate and then proceed to school, work, or other destinations. This short cut was not only exhausting, but rather dangerous, as it was in plain view of the opposing forces surrounding no man's land.

When skirmishes along the Al-Thawri/Abu Tor border became serious, we left our home for temporary safety in the same house in the Old City's Christian Quarter in which Futun and Khamis Sarsar resided when they adopted my father, George. We used one room of this old house, as the rest of it was rented.

My mother could no longer communicate with or reach her father, Jani, step-mother, Louisa, and most of her step-siblings in Katamon. That was also the case with the rest of the family in East Jerusalem, including the brothers and nephews of my grandfather and the two sisters of my mother's step-mother: Alexandra, married to "the German clockmaker," lived in Ramallah, and Lydia, married to the lawyer, Tahseen Kamal, lived in Nablus. Two of my mother's step-sisters lived in Jordan: Nadira, married to Louis Hanna Kafᶜity, lived in East Jerusalem, and Loreh, married to Fuad (Stawri) Daᶜdoush, a top Jordanian intelligence officer, lived in Amman. The only time we could see our West Jerusalem relatives was when they visited us once a year during Christmas. Like other Christians living in Israel, they were able to travel through Mandelbaum Gate—the only border crossing between Israeli West Jerusalem and Jordanian East

Jerusalem—in order to make the pilgrimage to Bethlehem, and stay for only two days.

My grandfather, my step-grandmother, one aunt, and three uncles numbered six of the 931 Christians who lived in West Jerusalem.[160] The stories they related to us about life in Israel did not fully register. Perhaps it was because we had no real context for what they were saying, or some of us were too young to absorb and integrate all the information we heard. What was memorable was the warmth created by their annual visit. Our grandfather was entertaining. Following his distribution of gifts, he would share with us anecdotes about living under the control of the Ottomans and serving for a short while in the British army during the British Mandate. He would imitate how British soldiers paraded inside Jaffa Gate by going back and forth in the living room, bellowing "lai ft" (left), "rig ht" (right) repeatedly like a British captain, and then saluting with his palm facing outwards.

The closure of the Government Printing Press left our father without work. He was only rehired three years later by the Greek Orthodox Patriarchal Printing Press. To make ends meet, our mother contacted Hana ʿAbla, her former teacher at the Swedish School, who was directing, at the time, the effort to provide clothing for Palestinian refugees. Hana obliged and began providing our mother with cut-up fabric. Using the Singer hand-crank sewing machine, she would assemble the pieces to make shirts and trousers. Working from home was a definite advantage, and our mother enjoyed it very much, as her simple creations served a good cause.

A Growing Family

My mother, and my grandmother and father by extension, stayed busy with raising the constantly growing family. In addition to my four siblings (Fatina, Anastasia, Khamis, and Michel) born in the 1940s, my mother gave birth to my third brother, Jamil, on Thursday, May 3, 1951. His name, meaning beautiful, arose not from an archangel's command, but rather from a jealous father's earnest question: "Why are your sons named after other relatives and saints? Why none of them is named after me?" Hence, Jamil was named after our maternal Greek grandfather, Jani Korfiatis, who became known in the community as Jamil al-Zayer.

I was next—the sixth child—born at Augusta Victoria Hospital, a Lutheran World Federation institution, on Tuesday, September 27, 1955. Coming into the world around the annual celebration of the Exaltation of the Holy Cross, I was named Saliba, derivative of *salib*, meaning cross or crucifix in Arabic. Tradition has it that St. Helena, Emperor Constantine the Great's mother, discovered the True Cross in 326 CE during her pilgrimage to Jerusalem.[161] Ever since birth, I have worn the Cross—my compass, my guide. Unlike my siblings, I am the only one not named after an angel, a saint, or a relative! Unlike my siblings, I am a caulbearer. I was born with a caul, a thin membrane that covered my whole body. My mother dried it and kept it. She said, "It will bring us all good luck."

Lucia, my youngest sister, who goes by the name Lucy, was born on Wednesday, July 15, 1959. Her name, meaning light, is not after a close or far away relative, but one of my mother's dear friends from Lebanon who visited her family in Jerusalem every summer.

My youngest brother, Elias, was born on Saturday, February 16, 1963—two days past Valentine's Day, not the Feast of Mar Elias that is annually celebrated on August 2. His name was chosen as a way of making up for missing the opportunity to do so fourteen years earlier when Michel was given his name. With his naming, our mother's promises were fulfilled. Heaven and Earth were at peace with each other!

Years later, my mother became pregnant again, for the last time, but had a miscarriage during the first trimester. I remember her wrapping the two fetuses in a white, linen cloth and my father burying the tiny bundle under the olive tree in our garden. For decades, my mother held a sacred dialogue as her hands caressed the leaves. Her fingers reached to Heaven to receive light green, dark green, dusty fruits of life. The tree, responding, bestowed bitter, sweet love to fall into my mother's palm, a communion of peace—forever.

My family was large. Not that my parents were competing with the other parents in the neighborhood, but each of the Salhab and Al-Tawil families had eleven children; each of the Al-Rishek and Zuᶜaiter families, ten; the Al-ᶜAtari family, nine; and the Abu Snineh family, eight.

An Unforgettable Experience

As the family grew, my father's monthly salary of six Jordanian dinars was barely sufficient to support the family. My mother sought work outside the house—uncommon in those days, particularly in Al-Thawri. A job opened up at the United Nations Relief and Works Agency (UNRWA) for Palestinian Refugees in the Near East. "It was God sent," as my mother often said. UNRWA was created by the UN General Assembly, following the 1948 Arab-Israeli War, to provide direct relief and work programs for Palestine refugees. "The Agency's services encompass education, health care, relief and social services, camp infrastructure and improvement, microfinance and emergency assistance, including in times of armed conflict."[162]

The job description was to supervise sixty tailors who made refugee clothing, two drivers, and porters. The test was to sew a pair of pants and a shirt, which my mother did many times before when she worked with Hana ᶜAbla. The salary was thirty dinars per month, five times the salary that my father earned in those days. This job was truly tailor-made for my mother, and she became supervisor at UNRWA in the fall of 1959. Working closely with her team, she raised morale and improved quality and production. Her director, Wadiᶜa Abu Dayyeh, was so impressed that she asked her to start offering workshops on sewing in Palestinian refugee camps to those wishing to learn.

A few months later, my mother was approached by a newly-hired employee, purportedly a former teacher, who offered her some 5000 dinars (an astronomical amount in those days, equivalent to over thirteen years of her salary) in exchange for lending him the warehouse key for one night only. She laughed it off, and nothing came of it.

It was several weeks later that my mother got the shock of her professional life. Upon opening the door to the warehouse one early morning, she found out it was totally empty. Bales and bales of fabric were all gone. The director and the inspectors rushed to investigate, but there was no trace of the tons of material. My mother felt awkward and responsible. She was speechless, until she noticed footprints coming out of the men's bathroom. The residue on the floor was starch powder generated by the cutting and tearing of the fabric.

It was then that my mother remembered the conversation she had with the new employee. Upon interrogating him, he confessed. The story: the employee entered the warehouse from the bathroom door he rigged to open the day before. He had seven conspirators, including two seamstresses and the guard. The stolen fabric was in a huge truck parked a few blocks away. All eight conspiring employees were summarily fired.

My mother stopped working at UNRWA in the summer of 1962. She became pregnant with Elias, and her gynecologist advised against exhaustion and stress.

A Tough Decision

Between Lucy's birth in 1959 and Elias's birth in 1963, we had a major family event, with great fanfare and joy, but one tinged with anxiety and sadness as well. In May 1961, unexpected guests arrived at the house, wanting to meet my parents and my seventeen-year old sister, Fatina, who was graduating from high school that year. It turned out they were wife shopping. This was not the first time for these types of visits. As per Palestinian social customs and traditions at that time, the mother or a close female relative of the groom-to-be would explore the possibility of marriage by speaking to the mother of the bride-to-be. If there is interest, and if the groom-to-be is found to be "from an honorable family," with sound reputation and a good profession (that is, the groom will be able to provide for his wife and family), then additional visits and a chaperoned courtship take place. If all goes well, wedding arrangements are made.

In Fatina's case, the close female relative who knocked at our door was Hanneh Nusnas. The groom-to-be was Salvador ("Sito") Kafati, and where he lived posed a challenge in those days. When he was two years old, his parents, Issa Kafati Bader and Caterina Cassis Hanneh, took him and his siblings from Beit Jala, the neighboring town to Bethlehem, to Honduras in Central America. Thirty years later, he returned to Beit Jala to marry a Palestinian Christian girl. In addition to being thirteen years older than my sister, he had no intention of staying in East Jerusalem or anywhere close. His next stop was San Pedro Sula. After my father inquired about, or rather investigated, his background—which was difficult to do, as everyone Sito knew lived in Honduras—he spoke to Fatina, and she accepted the idea of marriage. In contrast, my mother raised basic objections: Fatina was too young, and Honduras was too far from Jerusalem or, more specifically, "it was at the end of the earth." In 1961, Al-Thawri had no electricity, no telephones, and no televisions, and there was no easy way to reach Fatina in case of an emergency. The same applied to her connecting to the family, as Honduras was still developing.

Fatina wanted to get married, and threatened to become a Roman Catholic nun if my parents did not approve! Although that was not a good enough reason to become a nun, and she knew it, the lines separating the Christian denominations then were stricter than they are today. Most faithful in one denomination were not as readily receptive to losing one of their members to the other denomination.[163] Some 2000 years later, Jesus shakes his head in disbelief, asking: "What has gone wrong?"

A festive engagement followed in our garden in Al-Thawri. Family, friends, and neighbors celebrated for hours. A month later, Fatina and Sito were married on Thursday, June 29, 1961, in an equally festive religious ceremony at the Joachim and Anne Greek Orthodox Church in the Old City, near St. Stephen's Gate or Lions' Gate. A week later, the whole family stood by the entrance to our home, saying goodbye to the newlyweds. They set out on their life journey together—beginning with a one-month trip through Egypt, West Germany, and New York, en route to Honduras.

Long before the wedding cake was all eaten, a cloud of depression hovered over our home for a few weeks. My mother had the hardest time adjusting to Fatina's absence. Her work at the UNRWA helped a little, and her anxiety began to subside as letters and photos began arriving on a regular basis from Fatina. We would sit around to hear updates about life conditions in San Pedro Sula and the growth of her family. Communication became far easier with the arrival of electricity and telephones to our home. My mother accumulated all of Fatina's letters. A blue ribbon ties them together.

Tough Times, Pleasant Times

My parents made us feel comfortable—normal even—under abnormal conditions. We felt satisfied, even though we were relatively poor. The credit goes to our mother, who knew how to tailor clothes from older sister to younger sister and from older brother to younger brother. She was fair in allocating food and drink among the family members.

My mother and grandmother also baked cookies; made tomato paste, jams, and pickles; and harvested olives from our olive tree and cured them. They bought and dried *mulukhiyah* (mallow leaves) to be cooked with meat and rice throughout the year. A woman came once a year to prepare couscous. She did it the traditional way, by mixing semolina with water and rolling it with her hands for hours to create small pellets that were then dried and readied for consumption at a later date. Couscous was usually served with meat and vegetables.

To save money, my parents also kept a hen-house, a few rabbits, and a pigeonry in an enclosure at the far-left corner of our garden. As children, we loved collecting the chicken eggs. We had fun feeding the animals and playing with them.

Competition came from a garden snake, approximately five feet in length, which lived in the wild brush of the field below our garden. We, and the critters too, feared its color and waves. One time, it lashed at my grandmother, causing her right hand to swell. Whatever poison was used was not poisonous enough for the snake. The June 1967 War put an end to our animal collection, but my mother reported seeing smaller successor snakes in recent years.

As a family, we were raised on eating lamb. On Holy Pascha (commonly referred to as Easter), we always had lamb's head and shank or rib roast, along with stuffed grape leaves. On other occasions, some of the animals we raised unfortunately became our lunch or dinner. We always had a rooster on New Year, usually presented at the table, with its head on and a daffodil or narcissus flower in its mouth. The decoration had nothing to do with the myth of Narcissus or the moral that egotism and vanity often lead to dead ends, but was, rather, the result of my mother's artistic bend. New Year signified a new beginning and an earnest hope for peace, which my parents symbolized by opening every window in the house, placing an olive twig atop of each, and putting the light on in every room.

As a family, we were raised to drink tea. I am not sure if our parents were thinking of its health benefits at that time, or it was a matter of habit. Our father, "the tea maker," mostly used Ceylon black tea, as opposed to green or white tea, long before the small island of Ceylon in the Indian Ocean was renamed Sri Lanka in 1972. He would buy the tea loose leaf from Al-Hajj Munib on El-Khanka Street in the Christian Quarter. Sometimes, courtesy of my brother Michel, we would have Darjeeling or Earl Grey tea.

Whenever breakfast and dinner times came, my father would perform the tea-making ritual: boiling fresh water in the kettle, placing a little amount of boiled water into the decorative porcelain teapot to warm it and then pouring it out, filling the teapot with boiling water over three or four tea spoons of loose tea leaves, covering the teapot with its embroidered cozy to retain the heat and give the tea enough time for brewing and infusion. As children, we often added milk to the tea, a practice probably inherited from British times. We rarely drank Arabic (or Turkish) coffee, which was also bought at Al-Hajj Munib. That was usually offered, along with chocolate, to guests after meals or nearing the end of their visits.

My sister, Anastasia, and I especially loved to read. Perhaps we inherited this enjoyable lifetime habit from our parents. With borrowed books from a few libraries in and outside the city wall, my parents read about royal intrigues, such as the life and times of Roman Empress Flavia Maxima Fausta, the adventures of D'Artagnan in *The Three Musketeers* by Alexandre Dumas and Auguste Maquet, *kitab 'alf layla wa-layla* (*One Thousand and One Nights*, known in English as the *Arabian Nights*), *Rubá'iyát of Omar Khayyám*, and works by Daniel Defoe, Jonathan Swift, Robert Lewis Stevenson, Sinclair Lewis, and George Antonius, among others. They continuously encouraged me and my siblings to learn from the past and present, and our teachers especially. In a sense, they wanted us to take advantage of modern education and go further than they ever did. My father loved reciting the following Arabic verse, which he did from time to time, and I loved hearing him: "I honor my teacher far more than my parent // even though my parent provides me with fortitude and generosity. // The teacher educates the soul, which is the essence; // the parent enlivens the body, which is but a fragile shell."

In the days before we could afford a concrete patio, we had pebbles as surface for the walking areas of the garden of the seven fruits. One of us would carry a pan, and as we held each other by the shirt tail, we proceeded to follow certain pebble arrangements and pretend we were on a bus. From time to time, we stopped to let a passenger off or on.

Another game that got us into trouble was the creation of a banking system, with Khamis acting as President, and Anastasia as clerk with piles of coins created from foil wrappers of candies. The police came on one of their eternal quests for miscreants, communists, and socialists, and discovered the miniature bank. They were actually angry because we were creating competition to the obviously more sturdy banking system of the kingdom!

There were also moments when law violations were less humorous. We had a small, battery-operated radio strong enough to pick up broadcasts, not only from Jordan, but also Egypt, Syria, and Israel. While Egypt's President Abdel-Nasser was in power, important disagreements put him at odds with Jordan's King Hussein. As a result, the Jordan police would pass homes to listen, and if you were listening to anything other than the Jordan station, it was sufficient excuse for their intervention. As children will, we fought over our radio, and our father seized it in desperation and banged it against the wall. Whatever happened in that peculiar electronic age, the radio thereafter would receive only the Cairo broadcast, which, covered with a pillow, kept us out of legal trouble.

In addition to playing at home, we played in the neighborhood, even venturing at times into no man's land. I loved to climb the large fig tree to the south of the red house, located two streets below no man's land, to survey the landscape and watch passersby. My older brothers, Michel and Jamil, used to hunt for birds, or even turn over stones, as they searched for snails, especially around lent. While a yellow scorpion or two sometimes showed their claws and stingers and faced a certain death, most times, my brothers were successful in collecting three to four kilos of snails, which our grandmother and mother then purged and cooked with spices and spinach. Our parents always preferred snails from Jaffa, the ones grown on orange trees, but Jaffa was inaccessible between 1949 and 1967. I am happy to say that escargot à la spinach has not been part of my diet since that time.

Our playground included Wadi al-Rababeh. There are many rough places and caves—several of them lit by sunlight through cracks in the rocks. They were, at some point in time, utilized as tombs for the dead. One necropolis we knew well because it is part of the Greek Orthodox Monastery of St. Onuphrius,[164] still inhabited by Greek Orthodox nuns, where, in a particular section, one was affronted by dusty looking dogs that stand and growl at intruders in the midst of scattered human bones. Nearby is a traditional location where it is said Judas hanged himself. There are trees scattered throughout the land called the trees of Judas because they bear no fruit. At times, we would climb the side of the hill topped by the holy places above the Pool of Silwan. Our purpose was not religious, but rather part of a search for old Roman and Hebrew coins, especially after heavy rain. Michel was the best at it.

The Neighborhood

Until the late 1950s, the neighborhood had no running water. Water rationing was part of daily existence. I remember women carrying the empty, and later filled, buckets of water on their heads—a common practice for the transport of any goods, which has created a generation of people, regardless of age, who are erect as can be imagined, partly because of this exercise. Like Jacob's daughters, they found themselves seeking water at an intermittent spring down the valley. It is ironic since right below our garden passed the pipe that the Turks extended from "Solomon's Pools south of Bethlehem more than twelve miles across the hills to Jerusalem, converting an ancient tunnel under the Hill of Evil Counsel into a reservoir."[165]

Similarly, there was nothing but kerosene lamps or candles to light the interiors of the houses until the year of the miracle: 1964. "Let there be light" was brought into being by extending electric power to our neighborhood. The Siam brothers, two neighbors who worked for the electric company, made the connection. Recollections count the day of the coming of light coincidental with the visit of Pope Paul VI because it was overshadowed by a cultural sense of beings, seen and unseen.

The wind had howled more than usual through the valley, and the trees twisted in the onslaught. There was a sudden death in the neighborhood and, with the advent of light, the inhabitants reacted in superstitious ways. It was part of growing up.

If electricity was a problem even after its miraculous appearance, the telephone was enough to send one to Daheisha—the local hospital for the imbalanced! We had one of the first telephones in the neighborhood, and at any time, one might rap on the door and a request to use the phone. Sometimes, it would be a call to a son studying in Europe. No payment was ever asked for or given, which did not help the outrageous bills. Lines got mixed, or the phone failed completely. It was said that it was easier to grab a camel or a donkey and ride to Bethlehem because it could be done in a shorter time than trying to reach that modest city by telephone!

The arrival of electricity and modern refrigeration was joined by the increase in local, small businesses in the two streets below our house: grocery stores, an ironing shop, and a café. From the mid to the latter part of the 1960s, males—young and old—would congregate often at the café to watch black and white TV shows, especially boxing and wrestling matches. Following June 1967 and into century's end, the inhabitants mushroomed and so did businesses, including a bakery, a butcher's shop, mini markets, restaurants, a pharmacy, a beauty salon, a clothier, a library, an Israeli government-run health clinic, taxi service, and a couple of garages. Without proper city or neighborhood planning, each street became a parking lot, sometimes resulting in quarrels over space. Garbage increased as well, and unlike Turkish, British, or Jordanian times, there were no longer garbage collectors; people had to deposit their own garbage in large garbage containers. Unfortunately, the trash often found itself on the streets.

Our road remained dirty, stony, and unpaved for years. Its neglect was most inexplicable and surprising, given that it was shared by all and constantly used or abused. It was not only our passageway, but also our playground. When the road was paved finally in 1985, I was totally annoyed to learn that the bulldozers, with little sense of history, not only leveled the ground, but also tore away the two wells that had been used for a long time by several neighbors.

During the early morning hours, mothers or their daughters (if not in school) would clean sweep outside the main entrances to their abodes. Sometimes, you would hear female shouting, as dirty water found itself spilling over from entrance to entrance down the slight incline. It often spilled on our tiled entry way, but there were no altercations.

We had a neighbor who had made the required Hajj to Mecca. He has long since gone to his particular paradise, but we remember him because he insisted that he often saw a jinn or ghost under his grape arbor—which was, incidentally, also the location of the squat or the traditional toilet, Middle East style, with a pair of stone footprints aptly placed in juxtaposition to a hole in the ground. According to record, he was afraid to go to the toilet after dark. His good wife was a very outward person and would spend a goodly portion of the day going from kitchen to kitchen, drinking coffee or tea and catching up, or contributing to, the latest gossip, while continuously smoking cigarettes. With the passage of the observer of the jinn, she took an oath as a means of mourning to speak to no man, and many of us males who had been close to her found ourselves greeted with a blank and teary stare.

Prior to the early 1970s, television was still a part of the world of fantasy and the privilege of the rich. Children in the neighborhood entertained themselves by forming cliques that played soccer, hide and seek, and marbles. Boys played with boys and girls with girls. This usually happened during holidays or after school, which made grownups, especially females, sit outside the main entrance to their homes to keep watch over their children. When men passed by, women would retreat into their homes, and then reappear to continue the gossip or watch.

8
OUR NEIGHBORS, OUR FRIENDS

By the shadow of no man's land,
I notice friends within are not
welcome without. Strangers from
without are not welcome within.
Friends and strangers are separated
by hideous barbed wire, cement
walls, and war machines.

By the Lion's Fountain in Liberty Bell Park,
I notice friends within are welcome without.
Strangers from without are welcome within.
Friends and strangers are joined
by blood and flesh, by common sense.
No striking cement walls or barbed wire
separate us. We stand united.

Unlike family members, neighbors and friends are seldom inherited. They are usually made or chosen—sometimes intentionally and other times, not so intentionally. They walk into our lives, and we walk into theirs, starting a new path toward some unknown future.

Unlike legal relationships such as marriage, contacts with neighbors and friends live on or fade away without formal contracts. No religious authority or court official needs to officiate. Neighbors and friends remain if they want and separate if they want. Their commitment rests with how intensely they feel about each other and what that feeling and its context mean to them. Obviously, strong disagreements or opinions can disrupt a friendship, but not always.

Ideally, neighborliness and friendship rest on knowing others in their own uniqueness and not simply as an extension of one's experience. It ought not to take for granted but to take into consideration. It ought not to restrict and dictate but to liberate. It ought to empathize, not to ignore. It ought to stand not for ill, but for understanding and wholeness.

Neighborly Relations in Al-Thawri

The houses on our El-Kubanieh Road had no numbers for decades. These were not assigned until early 2016 and the road became an extension of Ein Rogel. Every neighbor, however, knew most of the names of the other neighbors and their pursuits.

It is amazing that over two generations, the two dozen or so families who lived on El-Kubanieh Road lifted themselves up socio-economically through ambition and hard work. Among their sons and daughters have been five doctors, a pharmacist, an accountant, four upholsterers or *munajdin*, a café owner, a carpenter, an electrical engineer, four bus drivers, two taxi drivers, a florist, a shoemaker, three teachers, and several grocers. My family has included one Catholic nun, one international civil servant, three businessmen, one social worker, and yours truly, a professor. Clearly, beyond the gender, national, professional, and religious backgrounds each of us embodies, the ideal that we must all attain is "the only identity and name worth seeking—that of human being.[166]

More Muslim Palestinian families from Hebron moved to Al-Thawri in the 1950s onwards. Over time, my family absorbed the Hebronite dialect and could shift in and out of it, as appropriate. Hebronites start their speech with low tones, extend their vowels, and stress certain syllables. Their vocabulary contains different names for items than people coming from other cities or regions; for instance, *tabliah* for dining room table instead of *alsoffrah*, *shezlong* for chaise lounge instead of *knabayah*, and *allhashah* for pillow instead of *mkhaddah*. My sister, Anastasia, who became a Catholic nun was best at it. At the Saint Joseph Hospital in Sheikh Jarrah, where she lived and worked for over three decades, patients from Hebron or Jerusalemites originating from Hebron, loved to call her "the Hebronite nun."

In the mid-1960s, my ten-member family—comprising one third of the Christian population that lived in the neighborhood among over three thousand Muslims—was easy to identify. We looked, dressed, and behaved differently. Our father, always wearing a suit and tie, was the most elegant man in the neighborhood. We were referred to as the Christian family. This title was both a blessing and a curse. For instance, we rarely needed to give detailed directions to visitors. They only had to ask for us. Occasionally, we ended up with supposedly lost tourists. Such cases of mistaken identity pleased us tremendously, and we felt at least partly needed.

In reality, we were needed even more, especially our mother, when the neighbors' health was concerned. Having learned how to give injections at the Augusta Victoria Hospital—interestingly enough, by practicing on a pillow—she was thought of as "the nurse" and consulted frequently. People used to knock at our front door past midnight, suffering from a "severe" stomach ache or wanting medication. Our mother knew the limits and stuck to what she was trained to do. She was both deft and light-handed, and the neighbors highly respected her. She charged two piasters (a piaster is one hundredth of a pound), if at all, per injection. Similarly, our ability to speak, read, and write in English and French, in addition to Arabic, induced some neighbors to ask for our assistance in translating and writing responses to letters from abroad, or giving a crash course in English prior to a high school final exam.

Helping neighbors did not always produce lasting effects. As the family evolved and each of us siblings flew the nest, my parents went through some unpleasant experiences. They had a couple of break-in incidents. My mother's small car was often a target of mischief, with windshield wipers twisted and four tires flattened. Cameras installed outside the house—which were later shot at and destroyed—successfully captured the image of the culprit, but my mother refused to file charges. As she explained, reiterating what my grandmother often said, "I was here first, long before most of them were even born. They are *all* my children." My mother's handbag was stolen from her as she was returning home one evening. When she informed a few of the neighbors, their response was "*haek ʿalaina*" ("your right is on us"), meaning "we take responsibility and we will remedy the situation." The bag was returned to her two days later, with everything in it except the house keys, which necessitated changing the main lock.

A case that wins the prize for dishonesty had to do with a neighbor who has since moved out. When our neighbor, Abu Ghazi, died, his family put up the house for sale. My eldest brother, Khamis, bought it. Following renovations, he rented it to foreign nationals, including United Nations personnel, who lived in the house on and off during a period of two decades. When the First Intifada (Palestinian uprising against the Israeli occupation) started in December 1987, the house became vacant, as foreign nationals were reluctant to rent in Palestinian neighborhoods such as Al-Thawri. Conditions were viewed as unpredictable, if not dangerous. Although no one lived in the house, and no water was consumed except for watering the garden, the monthly water bill remained high. Appeals reached dead ends. Eventually, the puzzle was solved. The neighbor on the other side of Khamis's house tapped into the water pipe of Khamis's house and siphoned water for several years before being detected. He denied any responsibility and argued that it must have been the prior owners who had been long deceased: his own parents!

My family was not constantly hassled or taken advantage of by neighbors. The holy days or holidays habitually brought out the best in our relationships. In preparation for the Christmas season, for example, we visited the Istanbouli family, whose property overlooked the Valley of Hinnom. With a saw in hand, we would cut a healthy and well-shaped branch of a pine tree from their expansive backyard and then cart it off up the hill and through the neighborhood for decoration. Neighbors would visit to wish us a "Merry Christmas and a Peaceful New Year."

During *Ramadan* (the ninth and holiest month in the Islamic lunar calendar, during which Muslims fast from sunrise to sunset, and fasting or *sawm* is one of the Five Pillars of Islam), we felt the excitement and witnessed the discipline, faithfulness, patience, sacrifice, and sense of community of our neighbors as they fasted and prayed. After the firing of the cannon, announcing the *iftar* (the meal around sunset and the call to prayer when the fast is broken), several children, four or five, would go from door to door, reciting loudly their praises. We would open the door and listen to them. "If it were not for Saliba, we would not have come to visit you. So, open your bag and hand us some *halawa* and two plates of baklava." Then, one of them would shout, "May God keep his mother," and everyone would say, "Amin." "May God keep his father." "Amin." "May God keep his brothers and sisters." "Amin." Once the performance is done, one of us would hand them money or sweets.[167]

Before dawn, the *musaher* (the person, always a male, who wakes up those observing Ramadan to remind them to have their meal before starting the day's fast), with drum and stick, would roam the streets and call upon the faithful to wake up, praise Allah, and welcome Ramadan, the month of forgiveness. We woke up as well, but most often returned quickly to sleep. We looked forward to eating *qatayef* (a kind of Arab light pancake filled with sweet cheese or nuts and spices and drenched in sugar syrup), sold only at that time of year, and to wishing our neighbors ʿ*Eid Mubarak* (a blessed holiday).

Our neighbors were not always amicable toward each other. In fact, their fights were harsh and sometimes bloody. Children-instigated family feuds, conflict over land rights, disagreements over wedding arrangements, and disrespect for someone's elders have sometimes incited not only heated arguments, but, moreover, drove some to brandish pocket knives.

Another paradox in our relations with our neighbors was to be called on to break up fights or even arbitrate a serious dispute—the assumption was that we did not have a partisan stake in the outcome of the altercation. A tragedio-comic situation took place when two brothers from a family up the street went at it with ample splashing of blood. Their mother dragged me to intervene. As I tried to do so, one of the two protagonists looked up at me and welcomed me home from a trip abroad and then set upon his sibling with a bloody stick.

There were, clearly, exceptions to the rule. Crises tended to generate in our neighbors' hearts a sense of communal responsibility and sharing. Many times they disregarded their differences and overextended themselves to ameliorate a certain situation. Whenever sickness struck or death occurred, scores of neighbors would genuinely offer, in addition to moral support, financial and physical assistance. How can I forget the morning when people rushed to rescue a neighbor's teenage daughter whose dress caught on fire? The experience was deadly. As shouting turned into screaming, and as women wailed, it became apparent that the worst had happened. Heard were religious cries: "la ilaha illa Allah wa Muhammadan rasulullah" ("There is no god but God and Muhammad is the messenger of God") and the familiar phrase "hathihi mashi'atu Allah" ("This is God's will"). Devoid of its religious content, what is so special about such a reaction? Humans anywhere react the same way to similar tragedies. Of a general certainty, but in our neighborhood specifically, tragedy was both felt and shared. It usually brought forth neighborly concern and empathy.

Another crisis that tested two families in our neighborhood, and busied others in thinking about it, relates to a case of consent and consensual sex, as well as interreligious marriage. Two of our young neighbors, a male and a female, must have entered into an amorous relationship, which is normal and happens regularly on the streets of Jerusalem and beyond. There were, however, serious complications: the female was Christian, and the male was Muslim. Even though one can think of several conjugal relationships, marrying outside one's religion in Jerusalem was, and still is, counter to societal expectations and tradition.[168]

When the Christian parents learned from their daughter about the illicit affair, they hit the ceiling. Dating without engagement and having sex before marriage were, and are, unacceptable. Their daughter, refusing to divulge who among the men from the Muslim family was the culprit, made things more difficult. They sought the direct intervention of Daoud Abu Ghazaleh, the *Muhafiz* (Jordanian civil governor of Jerusalem), who then summoned to his office all the men from the Muslim family. Upon finding out who was responsible, he summoned the sheikh to officiate at the wedding ceremony of the young couple, thus precluding further complications.

Living a few houses away from us, the couple had a good life and several children. They were among the first to arrive at Mar Elias (Prophet Elijah or Saint Elias) Monastery to attend my wedding in July 1996. When the husband suffered from kidney disease, his wife's generous gift extended his seasons and ease. When she suffered from cancer, he extended to her his support and love. Though facing death, they were pleasant, greeting passers-by from their second-floor balcony each afternoon till night. They were laid to rest, forty days apart, at the Muslim cemetery outside the Golden Gate to wait for the weighing of souls and the final bright light.

Like premarital sex, extramarital sex is equally disallowed in Islam and Muslim Arab culture. It constitutes *zina* or sin. In addition to its religious prohibition, its practice is viewed as a dishonor, often dealt with by a male member or members of the aggrieved family.

Growing up, we—our father and five of us boys—neither went to a barbershop nor had long hair. A barber who lived down the valley from us visited with us every two months. It was usually a pleasant experience, as we watched him cut our hair and converse about the latest news from near and afar. One day, he disappeared. His family located his dismembered body days later. His crime: extramarital relationship. We never learnt who did it and what happened to the person, nor did we want to know. What is important is that while customs and traditions have value, they must not be used to contravene people's civil, cultural, economic, political, and social rights. While unsanctioned acts must stop, taking the law into one's one hand is equally wrong. Honor can never be found in honor killing.

The New Neighbors Next Door

In August 1968, a Western-looking young man moved next door to my house. I helped him carry his belongings: paintings, sculptures, tools, and not much else. He was a twenty-seven-year-old artist, fresh from art school in London. I was a twelve-year-old, fresh from experiencing the June 1967 War. I made nothing of assisting him; it was an act of courtesy, plain and simple. It took me a few weeks to realize that he was an Israeli Jew from across no man's land. The enemy from beyond the border was actually living next door. Although the border had been dismantled by then, I was still dependent on it and on national and religious distinctions. Like others in the neighborhood, I greeted him and we smiled, but my act of friendship was just that: an act. Politeness and respect for others were integral parts of my upbringing.

In October 1968, a young woman moved in with him. Blonde and tall, and sometimes with short skirts and sleeveless tops, her walk was rarely ignored. Fully clad, tradition-bound Palestinian women took a second look whenever she passed, let alone men in general. It was equally strange to see "the new couple on the block" hold hands in public. While much had changed since, it was not customary for women and men to be affectionate outside their homes.

My unspoken apprehensions about our next-door neighbors were not long lived. After months of passing each other on the road, we stopped being mere faces or just neighbors, but actual people with names. When I met Israel and Brigitte, something surpassing the border developed. In difference, we became familiar. Perhaps it was our curiosity to know each other's world. Perhaps it was our common need to overcome enmity, to affiliate and belong. They definitely did not need a boy in their lives, and I had my family, my schooling, and little time for them. Decades later, I feel blessed to have had and still have Israel and Brigitte and their two sons, Noam and Jonathan, as my closest Jerusalem friends.

Once friendship took root, the border totally disappeared. Our hardships and joys became one and the same. This was true, irrespective of all the challenges, outright antagonism, and suspicions that separated Palestinians from Israelis: the Israeli Jewish tendency not to trust Palestinians; the Palestinian attitude not to mingle seriously with Israeli Jews; Palestinian attacks inside Israel; maltreatment of Palestinians in the West Bank and the Gaza Strip; Israeli settlement policy; and so on. While we recognized the contentious issues, our focus remained on what was common to us. We did not work at it; it just happened that way. This is not to say either of us agreed with or condoned decisions from above and events occurring around us.

Israel, the son of Jewish immigrants from Poland, was born in Afula during the British Mandate. He is unimpressed by politics and politicians. His primary attention is on his family and his art.[169] He lives and breathes creativity. Working as a sculptor, he spends hours perfecting his sketches and designs. Among Israel's most distinguished artists, Israel is "the master." His sculptures are on exhibit in Israel and throughout the world, in addition to his Judaica art.

Israel the creator was also Israel the soldier. Moments of doubt occasionally drew me back to the border, especially when he had to perform his annual military service. I questioned if he was stationed in the West Bank or the Gaza Strip, or if he was guarding posts along the border with adjacent Arab states. This became concrete during the October 1973 War and Israel's invasion of Lebanon in 1978 and 1982. I wondered if he was in harm's way. Conversely, I wondered if he was causing harm to others, mainly those on my side of the border. Nevertheless, I ultimately realized that his side and my side of the border were one and the same.

I drew much strength from Brigitte who married Israel. Born and raised in Germany, she found it initially difficult to live in a "strange" Palestinian neighborhood of Al-Thawri and adjust to Israeli-Jewish life. We unconsciously constructed meaning and order of the world around us. We built bridges toward each other's worlds. I provided assurance, friendship, and predictability; she enhanced my love of reading, empathy, and wisdom.

When Brigitte gave birth to Noam (Chico) and Jonathan (Joni), we celebrated. My family welcomed the Hadanys with open arms. My home became their home. Chico and Joni called their mother "ima" and my mother "mama." They ate our food, and we partook in their joy and sadness. They got to know the Palestinian neighbors. When Chico and Joni performed their annual military service, I knew how they would treat others: with respect.

Israel, Brigitte, and I made frequent trips to the Old City, visited the holy sites of the three Abrahamic faiths, and loved to drink Arabic tea or Turkish coffee and share *kaek bil simsim*, *falafel*, and *humus* on countless occasions. We usually shopped for food together on Fridays and then enjoyed cheese *bourekas* pies and *café hafuch* or "upside-down"—similar in taste to cappuccino—with a piece of chocolate, at cafés in Jerusalem.

Israel and Brigitte introduced me to art and environmental design. I was their guide to Palestinian culture. Due to our relationship, I became interested in the conciliatory thought of Rabbi Judah Leon Magnes, the dialogic philosophy of Martin Buber, the humanistic poetry of Yehuda Amichai, the peace poetry of Ada Aharoni, and the works of authors like Amos Oz, A.B. Yehoshua, and David Grossman. I got to appreciate even more Palestinian commitment and creativity in the lives and works of the national poet Mahmoud Darwish, Latin Patriarch of Jerusalem Michel Sabbah, theologian Rafiq Khoury, educator and legislator Hanan ͨAshrawi, community activist Nora Kort, philosopher Sari Nusseibeh, sociologist Bernard Sabella, artist Soleiman Mansour, and actress Hiam Abbas, among many others. In addition to being a famed sculptor, Israel is a published poet. He read his poems to me, and I read my poems to him and Brigitte. They have been as proud of my accomplishments as I have been of theirs.

Out of conflict, a genuine friendship between "enemies" evolved and has survived the Palestinian-Israeli tragedy. It is stronger amid the impasse, injustice, and violence. However, a valid argument can be made that this is the exception, like other interracial or interreligious relationships that have transpired in different parts of the world: Catholics and Protestants in Northern Ireland; African Americans and Whites in the United States; Sunni and Shi ͨa Muslims in Lebanon; and Ashkenazi and Sephardic Jews in Israel. I agree, but up to a point. When the chips are down, most people part ways. They tend to revert to what is basic, certain, immediate, and socially acceptable. This is especially applicable when one's life is in danger, one's socioeconomic wellbeing is in jeopardy, or one's reputation is on the line.

Over the years, the Hadanys and I have learned that when relationships are anchored in circles of asymmetrical power or enmity, they remain unequal and disadvantaged relationships. They have little chance of flourishing if one party to them has no choice but to acquiesce. However, when relationships rise above the expedient and the pragmatic, they have a chance to grow. We have learned that people from across borders must constantly fight the urge to take each other for granted. To live peace, people must be willing to take risks for peace. Clearly, friendships cannot be imposed; they must grow from the heart. While such growth takes time, it is important to take the opportunity to initiate them. It is beneficial and healthy to envision them. Thinking of the dream we want to become is vital.

After twenty years as neighbors, the Hadanys left al-Thawri for the German Colony or Moshava Germanit, a ten-minute walk away—which is now predominantly Jewish, in contrast with the pre-1948 period when it was home to Christian Arab families and, before that, to members of the Templer sect from Württemberg, Germany. As I was away living and working in the United States, my mother asked Israel and Brigitte to relocate because of the charged atmosphere in al-Thawri and the region. The First Intifada was taking shape in 1987-1988.

Today, as in the past, the Hadanys and I wish for a better tomorrow, not only for our children and grandchildren, but for all Palestinians and Israelis. Our future rests not with dispossession and disempowerment, but with reclaiming dignity and hope for all. Relationships like ours are the building blocks of caring, of community, of real peace.

Abu Tor/Al-Thawri: A Tale of Two Neighborhoods

The disparities, stress, and fear that characterize aspects of life in Jerusalem and the region find echoes in corners of Abu Tor/Al-Thawri. When the former catches a cold, the latter sneezes!

Inhabited mostly by Christian and Muslim families before the establishment of Israel,[170] the neighborhood on the hill has become split over seven decades: an Israeli Jewish side in the west and a Palestinian Muslim side in the east, with a handful of Christians on each side, like my mother who has lived in al-Thawri since 1941. This split became solid in 1948-49, specifically when Israel began controlling its western part and Jordan its eastern part. Since 1967, while the neighborhood has become one geographically under Israeli jurisdiction, it remains divided demographically, culturally, and politically, contrary to the mixed residential neighborhood idea that is often touted in the media. Palestinians pass through Abu Tor on their way to and from other parts of Jerusalem, but Israelis are rarely seen passing through Al-Thawri. A main reason is fear of the other. This has been the case since the start of the First Intifada in 1987.

A tale of two neighborhoods is manifest. This starts in the middle, where Ein Rogel Street and Gikhon Street meet and where HaMetfaked Street in the north and Naomi Street in the south meet Abu Tor Street, as visible in Map 5. The latter street winds through Al-Thawri, until it connects with the recently named Maʿalot Ir David Street, just below Wadi Hilwa and the southern side of the Old City wall.

Abu Tor is home to Israelis, United Nations and European Union personnel, and other internationals. It is full but not overly crowded, with clean, tree-lined roads and lively gardens. It is well integrated into the Jerusalem municipal system. Its property is extremely expensive, given the amazing views of Mount Zion and the Old City; its proximity to entertainment, parks, promenades, and shopping; and the presence of two synagogues—one for Ashkenazi Jews and the other for Sephardic Jews. In contrast, Al-Thawri is home to Palestinian Muslims and has two mosques. It is congested, with its dirty roads looking like parking lots at nights, on Fridays, and on holidays. While it enjoys lush greenery and equally spectacular views, it suffers from major problems, including insufficient schools, a housing shortage, a poor street network, and weak infrastructure and services.[171] These deficits add to its vulnerability and make it less immune to radical tendencies and episodes of unrest.

In the past few years, there have been multiple episodes of mischief and even violence, with firm responses from the Israeli police and security apparatus. On April 7, 2013, a group of twenty Arab youth smashed the windows of some twenty Israeli Jewish cars in Abu Tor.[172] On October 31, 2014, Al-Thawri resident, Moʿtaz Hejazi, an Islamic Jihad operative, was killed by Israeli police for allegedly attempting to kill Rabbi Yehudah Glick, a right-wing Israeli activist and proponent of constructing the Third Temple.[173] During the week of July 27, 2015, the police arrested seven youths—three of whom are from Al-Thawri—for attacking Jews on a Jerusalem promenade in Jabal al-Mukabbir or Armon HaNatziv, founded in 1973 on territory captured during the June 1967 War.[174] These and other incidents make my mother retreat within her abode to light another candle for divine intervention. She prays for "the dark clouds to pass," for mutual understanding, and for peace to materialize. We do, too.

Map 5: Abu Tor/Al-Thawri

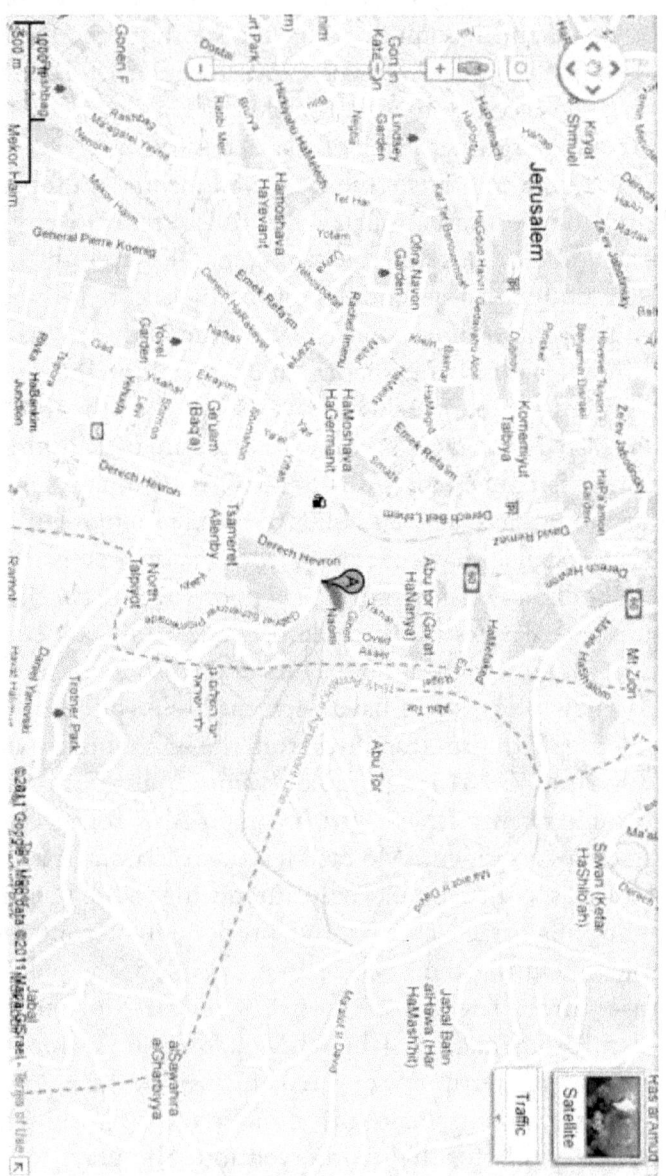

With all the differences between Abu Tor and Al-Thawri, it seems that the Israeli, mostly Jewish, and Arab, mostly Muslim, neighbors can find themselves sometimes on the same side when it relates to apolitical matters: parking, safeguarding green spaces, and fighting to preserve the integrity of the land surrounding the ancient Greek monastery on top of the Abu Tor hill. Why? Michael Steinhardt, an American financier and philanthropist, and David Sofer, a London-based Israeli businessman, have secured a one-hundred-ten-year lease from the Greek Orthodox Patriarchate to build a hotel and high-end apartments in the Greek monastery.[175] There is also a neighborhood women's group that meets to learn each other's cultures and languages. An Israeli Jewish woman teaches Hebrew, and a Palestinian woman teaches Arabic. The group goes on outings to locations such as the Jerusalem Botanical Gardens. Elana Rozenman, one of the group's leaders, told me, "It's always good for others to see us together in public and witness our sisterhood."

While the Palestinian-Israeli conflict must be resolved, it is incumbent upon those in authority to address the multiple daily challenges facing Jerusalem and her inhabitants, no matter their background, faith tradition, and political affiliation. Investing in neighborhoods equally and treating everyone equitably would ease tensions and empower many more people to care. Educating inhabitants to cooperate with and respect each other will promote real coexistence. Otherwise, there will be continued estrangement, injustice, and violence. That is how my family and countless others of good will feel.

9
FAMILY PROFILES

Like the limbs of
a living tree, we
—three sisters, five brothers—
connect to our main stem,
our common roots.
The same letter of the alphabet
neither starts nor ends

our given names,
our branches seek light
in different world corners,
but the Gardener is One.
No matter the distance apart,
no matter the time and space
between us, love is eternal.

We grew up in a traditional Middle Eastern home, built on the power of basic human values. However, real power was evidenced more in the domain of the political and the security apparatus. Our trust was more in faith and in what is just, legal, and right than in such power.

In our home, emphasis was put on compassion, empathy, forgiveness, kindness, respect, and sacrifice. We did not use the word "love" frequently, but rather strove to practice it by reaching out to help one another within our family, as well as the others around us. Hard work and accomplishment were highly prized.

Our grandmother, our mother, and our father were our exemplars, but so was our religious upbringing, both in church and at school. No one was trying to create "angels," "saints," or "stars" of us, but rather responsible human beings, capable of receiving and giving even more. Although there were instances of parental discipline, sibling rivalry, and jealousy, as is natural in most families, we—three sisters and five brothers—were treated fairly and liberally. Gender distinctions mattered little in our home, contrary to what existed in our local geography.

Within our family, our voices—our touches—counted and helped carry us through hard times. Neighborly relations, Arab-Jewish connections, and the Palestinian-Israeli impasse impacted all of us in various ways, and each of us had to come to terms with them and make sense of the living mosaic, Jerusalem.

Let me introduce you more closely to my individual family members, starting with my grandmother and parents, and then my sisters and brothers. (See Figure I for the Sarsar Family Tree. It consists of the Russian, Greek, and Palestinian Arab roots and spans four generations.)

Grandmother Futun

My "adoptive" grandmother, on my father's side, was of Arab Palestinian ethnicity. She toiled unlike any other during the eight decades she lived in Jerusalem. She loved the city and rarely traveled outside of her borders, but her experience there had been tough and full of challenges: a locust invasion in 1915; a major earthquake in 1927; four sets of governing authorities (Ottoman, British, Jordanian, and Israeli); an Arab revolt of 1936-39; seven subsequent Arab-Israeli wars; temporary displacement

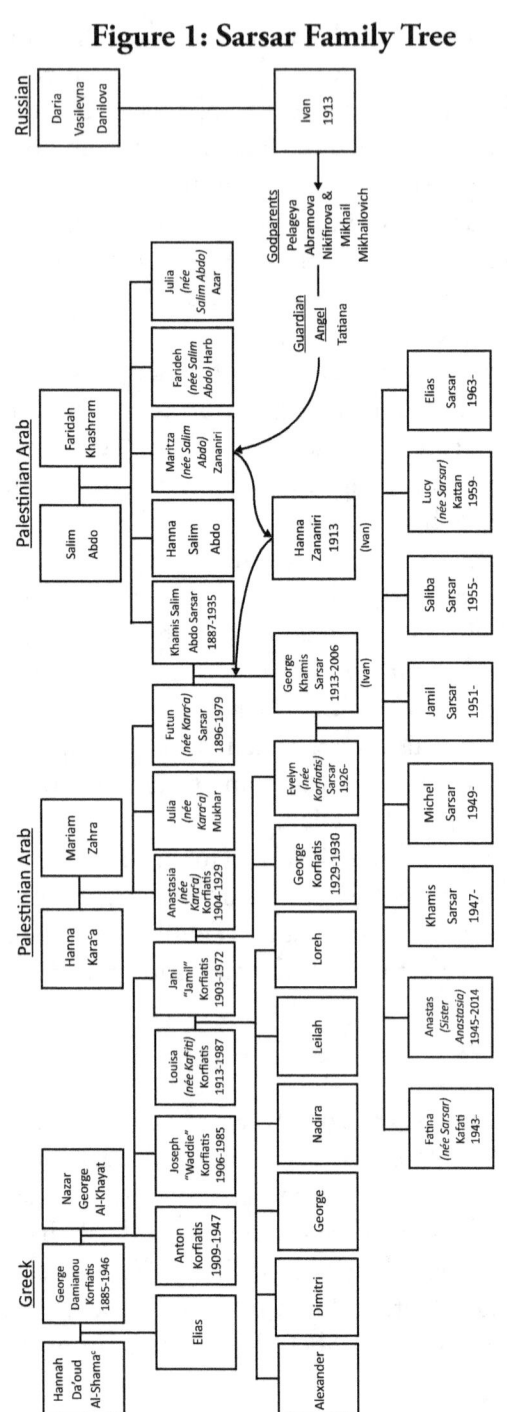

Figure 1: Sarsar Family Tree

during the 1948 and 1967 wars; and loss of her adoptive son, Hanna, from typhoid; the death of her sister, Anastasia, during childbirth; and the death of her husband, Khamis, from prolonged illness. In all, she remained sane and retained love for others.

My grandmother was like a second mother to all of us. She was a main pillar of our family, having adopted our father and fully embraced her niece—our mother, Evelyn. Although resolute, she was kind and totally dedicated to her family. She went beyond the call of duty to be of assistance and to guide us, without prying. When my mother worked for over two years at UNRWA, my grandmother was the one who ensured that the household routine was maintained.

"As a toddler," my grandmother used to tell me laughing, "you used to stomp on my back." As a lad, I felt my grandmother's firm grip as we shopped once a week in the Old City market for fresh fruits and vegetables. Her magical grand chef hands created delicacies, only to be consumed by the family in a few minutes.

During the week of major holidays, our grandmother and mother would make special cookies or desserts, and we, the children, would gather to help and reminisce about the "old days" and anticipate better days to come. While Christmas is special as it commemorates Jesus's birth, Easter week or Holy Week is equally special, as it embodies not only Jesus's crucifixion and burial, but also His resurrection. A favorite kind of sweets we looked forward to making and eating around Easter is *kaek and maʿmoul* (stuffed cookies with dates and nuts, respectively). In the Christian cultural tradition, the round kaek resembles the crown of thorns, the closed *maʿmoul* symbolizes the tomb, and the ingredients inside the *kaek and maʿmoul* and their sweet taste refer to resurrection.

One Good Friday, we made large quantities of *kaek wa maʿmoul*, which was time-consuming. Our grandmother guided us as we kneaded, rolled, stuffed, and decorated each individual piece with cookie tweezers. That was before we had molds with the different designs on them. Once finished, Nabil, the baker's son, picked up the several trays of *kaek and maʿmoul* for baking at his family's bakery nearby. I can still hear my grandmother's shrieks from that Friday as she received the trays back from Nabil. They contained a heap of broken cookies. The baker's payment: "May God burn your bones!" My grandmother had a saying befitting every occasion. Cookies or no cookies, Easter was celebrated. There is hope. Resurrection is the other side of crucifixion. Darkness gives way to a glorious light.

My grandmother died on Friday, September 28, 1979, one day past my twenty-fourth birthday. For some reason, my birthday meant a lot to her, which she always marked by baking one of her specialty cakes and by decorating with flowers the placemat where I ate. Perhaps I was one of her favorites. She was buried on Mount Zion in the same tomb as her sister, Anastasia, and her mother, Mariam. The tombstone confirms the years "1901-1979." However, her birth certificate, bearing the Ottoman crest, buried in her stack of paperwork, tells a different story. Her name there is listed as Noor, meaning light, which is what Futun also means, as it is from the Greek name Photini or light. Moreover, her birth year in the Hijri calendar is given as "1314," which converts to "1896" in the Gregorian calendar. Why she preferred the name Futun, instead of Noor, is a mystery. Why 1901 was used, instead of 1896, is equally a mystery. Was it a deliberate mistake or an honest clerical mistake? She probably did not care, but God only knows!

As children, my parents found caring and love in Futun, a mother who was not their own. Out of nothingness, wholeness and a sense of belonging were born. Out of empathy, perseverance, and sacrifice, they planted deep roots in Jerusalem's life.

My grandmother's oval portrait still hangs in the reception room of our home in Al-Thawri, above her embroidered cushions. Her penetrating gaze, her plump face, conveys a more serious than usual look, as if she is posing, but less stern than her husband in an adjacent portrait, with a curved moustache surpassing the sultan's and a fez on his head. Without them, my parents would definitely have had a different and, quite possibly, a harder life.

Father George

Like his adoptive mother, my father had a tough life, going through an endless series of conflicts and wars that adversely impacted him, his family, and his work. The typesetting job he did for some five decades, while fulfilling, was uneven and did not pay well. When he returned to it at the Greek Orthodox Patriarchal Printing Press following the June 1967 War, nothing had changed for him. He still had to typeset in several languages and several alphabets, although he would be the first to admit he was not always sure of all the script versions. He still had to meet print deadlines. His salary of twelve dollars per week did not increase. Like the ancient but well-preserved Gutenberg printing press he used, the dust, humidity, and metallic letters, all characteristic of his workplace, remained. His Greek boss, the Greek bishop above him, and the Greek Patriarch at their head stayed in position as well.

My father felt comfortable with this continuity. He had a high respect for authority and tradition. His conservative approach tended to be accented by his personality. Besides being caring, courteous, and quiet, he was cautious, frugal, and restrained. He had a long, long fuse. Unless deeply angered or hurt, sometimes even by an unkind word, he kept his composure.

Once my father's temper was triggered, it could become explosive, at least for a short duration. One example is offered. When we were children, my parents would buy watermelons by the dozen. Placing them under the bed, they believed, would keep them cool and fresh longer. My father usually opened the watermelons and followed the same ritual. A short baptismal of each always ended with *bismillah* (in the name of God in Arabic) and a circular cut at the top of the skin, as if shaving a friar's head. The red flesh would appear, feeling the light away from the summer sun. Vertical cuts from top to bottom would release that sweet aroma, soon revealing "the bride" at the center of watermelon creation. With home-baked bread and white cheese, lunch became a true celebration. One day, as a fight over the bride erupted between my two eldest brothers, my father—in exasperation—smashed bride and all against the white wall, causing red tears to flow and a big mess below.

Unlike the strategy of resolving the watermelon dispute, my father was apolitical, preferring to be a commentator or spectator, not a participant. Every morning, he listened to news from several sources, mainly the BBC and the radio stations of Jordan, Egypt, and Israel. When asked a historical question, he provided a thorough explanation of its relevance to prior ages and the role that leadership had played in bringing about change. He had a genuine concern for the human tragedy that had beset the region—a concern well informed by decades of living in Jerusalem and of pondering the lessons of history under Ottoman, British, Jordanian, and Israeli rule.

The several conflicts and wars my father experienced made him more critical and impatient with blind political extremism and the worsening of economic conditions. He did not understand why the "intelligent" leaders on both sides of Arab-Jewish and Palestinian-Israeli relations cannot be more imaginative and find a workable solution. He did not tolerate injustice. Military checkpoints and resultant delays angered him greatly.

My father loved beauty and nature. He devoted hours upon hours caring for our garden that, at times, looked like a greenhouse. While gardening is a wonderful opportunity to make flowers and plants grow and be beautiful, it poses some dangers for those who are allergic to pollen. My father had a serious allergy, and each spring, he experienced horrendous episodes of sneezing and coughing. Yet, his allergy never deterred him from pursuing his gardening. He always made sure to pick the most exquisite flowers and present them with love to my mother.

In later months and years, I frequented the Church of Sitna Mariam, where my orphaned father received a new life. His adoption story must have left a strong impression on my psyche. I needed to experience for myself the location and its spiritual powers. The church is located deep beneath Gethsemane. Entering its ornamented doorway, it takes a few seconds for one's eyes to adjust to the darkness inside. The transition is eased by the tens of lit candles indicating the way downward. The steps are slippery. The millions of candles that were lit over the years—including those of my relatives—have left their traces. Tapestry, lamps, and candles adorn the entire burial chamber. One of the several icons shows Mary's body surrounded by the apostles, while in the background, Christ holds in his hands the soul of Mary about to be taken to heaven. Like the age-old belief that Mary's body did not remain in the grave, my orphaned father found hope. Darkness and death were transformed into light and life.

My father passed away on July 21, 2006. Though he lived in the pain of loss and the shadow of conflict, he remained a kind man, winning countless friends across the ethnic, national, and religious divides. With hundreds of white roses and tulips atop a simple casket, Christians, Muslims, and Jews, Palestinians, and Israelis, delivered him to his last earthly abode on Mount Zion. He is buried in the same tomb as his adoptive father, Khamis, only a few yards away from his adoptive mother, Futun. His remains form part of the city's foundation. A job well done; a memory etched in stone and forever in my heart.

As an interesting aside, nearby is the tomb of George Habib Antonius, with the Arabic inscription that reads, "Awake, oh Arabs, and arise." Antonius, born in Cairo, Egypt, was a Greek Orthodox Christian of Lebanese origin. He engaged in public service under the British Mandate and authored the book, *The Arab Awakening*.[176] My father met him and read his book.

Mother Evelyn

My mother spent her life fully committed to the family. She sincerely acknowledged the love shown to her when her own mother passed away and reciprocated tenfold, especially when others were in dire need. When her own father Jani (or my grandfather) had a stroke and was frail, she looked after him daily at the Home for the Elderly in Abu Dis, even though he never fulfilled his promise of compensating her for the land he bought and the house he built with her mother's jewelry or money. He died in 1972. When her aunt or mother-in-law Futun (or my grandmother) became sick, she was the one who led the family effort to provide her with utmost care, comfort, and love. When her stepmother Louisa (Jani's second wife or my step-grandmother) contracted cancer and was placed at the Saint Louis French Hospital in Jerusalem, my mother, along with other members of the family, took her daily breakfast and kept her company. Louisa's children, or my mother's stepsiblings, lived abroad or were unavailable. Louisa died in my mother's arms in 1987.

My mother accommodated change more easily than my father. While equally caring and courteous, she is a fighter for whatever concerned the family, and for what is just and right. Along with our father and grandmother, she was able to create an environment for growth, happiness, and health in the face of tremendous money shortages and an unsure future in a land "between war and peace."

The conflicts and wars transformed my mother. With much commitment, energy, ingenuity, and quiet strength, she took a more active role outside the home at a time when society did not endorse such moves. She learned how to drive stick shift, and did so skillfully. Automatic transmission was too easy for her!

With us children all grown up—and with assistance from the family, especially my brothers, Khamis and Jamil—my mother became a business woman. In 1973, she opened a furniture store near Rachel's Tomb at the northern entrance of Bethlehem, and called it "Lucy," after my younger sister's name. For most customers, she became known as "Madam Lucy," Madam being a title of respect. The first pieces of furniture she sold included our dining room set. Within a couple of years, the business expanded. She did major deals with bamboo manufacturers in the Gaza Strip and foam importers in the West Bank. She bought bales of colorful fabric and, using her sewing skills, made living room and dining room cushions. Customers, domestic and foreign, flooded the store. Furniture orders came from far and wide: from regular folks in Ramallah and Tel Aviv, to diplomats and UN officials.

Business was disrupted in December 1987 with the start of the First Intifada or uprising against the Israeli occupation of Palestinian lands, which ended with the Madrid Conference in 1991 or, as some would argue, with the Oslo Accords of 1993. Israeli customers especially were too afraid to venture into Arab cities and neighborhoods. The Oslo peace process—which created the Palestinian Authority and brought Palestinian control to areas of the West Bank, including Bethlehem where the furniture shop was located—eased tensions, but was insufficient to improve business. My mother persevered, hoping for better days to come. Conditions worsened, and business came to a standstill with the Second Intifada during 2000-2005 and the construction of the Israeli security or separation barrier, with its checkpoints and watch towers. With no customers in sight, layers of dust on bamboo have dried up. I ask: "When will the barrier be brought down? When will business resume? When will dignity return to those who care?"

To my mother's mind, "the best government is one that treats its people fairly and does not meddle in their affairs, as long as they obey the law." High taxes and inflation rob people of their hard work and motivation. Peace is urgent, as it enables people to actualize themselves and help those around them.

My mother's faith has always been in God. She fasts and makes pledges so that He protects her children, seventeen grandchildren, and eight great grandchildren. She gave each of us children a small gold cross, with a mini chamber containing a tiny relic of the True Cross, and urged us to wear it: "This relic," she insisted, "was passed on to us from prior generations." She loves to light the daily candle and place fresh flowers, usually picked from our garden, in front of our favorite icon of the Resurrection. This icon is half burnt, from a lit candle that fell on it. It is surrounded by countless other icons and religious mementos, all placed on the wide windowsill.

My mother has also photos of the whole family decorating the reception room, or what we call the salon, the dining room, and her bedroom. She went so far as to create one or more photo album for each of us children, which are bulging at the seams.

Sisters

Fatina

My oldest sister, Fatina, is both gentle and kind. As the first child, she was showered with affection and attention, but not necessarily spoiled. Perhaps that is the fate of most first-born children. She loved wearing her school uniform, beret, white socks, and black shoes. This formal dress code at Saint Joseph School made her stand out. A couple of her classmates remember her as extremely well-behaved, or "a saint."

Attending Sunday Roman-Rite mass in Latin at the Church of the Holy Sepulchre was compulsory, but meaningful.[177] While Fatina did not appreciate the compulsory part, no one would, she appreciated the chanting and spiritual atmosphere. Following services, she would proceed to Mar Yaʿcoub (Saint James)—the parish church of the Arabic-speaking Greek Orthodox community—next door to the Holy Sepulchre, to join my parents for the remainder of the Greek Orthodox mass in both Arabic and Greek.

My father usually took Fatina to and from school, quite a bus ride from Al-Thawri to the Old City and back, and quite a brisk walk from Damascus Gate to Jaffa Gate and back. The way back home was more leisurely and interesting for Fatina, as my father stopped to shop or pick up last-minute goodies. In later years, she was the one to hold onto the hands of Anastasia, Khamis, and Michel, as they began their kindergarten in the Old City.

At home, my father helped Fatina with her geography and history homework. He even accompanied her on her school trips—for example, to Bethlehem and Jericho—since my mother was already busy with the household and caring for Anastas and Khamis. However, my mother assisted Fatina with math and science. My grandmother showed her how to embroider and cook.

Whenever Fatina wanted to do household chores, my mother would say to her: "Go study now. Your time for work will come." Education was paramount for my parents. They viewed it as a sure ticket to a better life. Their experience of constantly living on a limited income highlighted for them the need to secure knowledge and marketable skills. They wanted to provide Fatina, and the rest of us children, with the best education and opportunities that were not available to them.

While Fatina was excited to get married at age seventeen and explore the world beyond Jerusalem, she was deeply saddened by leaving Jerusalem, but comforted by the thought that she will remain in touch and return home to visit. She was sickened by the June 1967 War, worrying about our wellbeing from afar in San Pedro Sula, Honduras. She made many phones calls to relatives (since we had no telephone at that time) and wrote several letters. Even though apolitical in all respects, she often questioned the wisdom of reaching goals or resolving conflict through aggression and terror. She remains in Honduras where she is enjoying being with her grandchildren. Her husband, Sito, passed away on May 4, 2011.

Anastasia[178]

My second sister, Anastasia or Anastas, was not born a saint, but developed into one. As a child, she was fearless, protecting her older sister and speaking truth to power. As a teenager, she extended herself to help others and excelled at whatever she pursued.

Born in 1945, she was raised Orthodox Christian, but decided to become Roman Catholic, having been influenced by the Roman Catholic nuns at Saint Joseph School. Anastas's decision to join the order of Saint Joseph of the Apparition fell hard on some members of the family, especially my mother. The expectation was that she would marry, as was customary and as several young men showed interest. When the marriage angle did not succeed, my mother suggested that she becomes an Orthodox Christian nun instead.

Anastas's mind was already set, and the ordination took place. She ended with dedicating her life to caring for the sick at the Saint Joseph Hospital in Sheikh Jarrah in Jerusalem.

In retrospect, Anastas's decision should not have come as a surprise. When I was a child, she cared for me, since my parents and grandmother had to contend with the rest of my brothers and sisters. It was also customary in those days for elder sisters and brothers to take care of their younger siblings. Occasionally, I escorted Anastas on her weekly visits to homes for orphaned children and the blind. For her, it was the fulfillment of her moral, religious, or social obligation. Initially, I went along because of her request, but later, I participated out of a sense of doing the right thing. It grew on me. Although she was ten years my senior, I often accompanied her to Sunday mass, social parties, and shopping. In a sense, I was her bodyguard. It was tough for a young woman to grow up in Jerusalem, particularly in an all-Muslim neighborhood such as Al-Thawri. Muslim females of all ages were fully protected, and even though they travelled freely and securely, it was uncommon for them to arrive late at night unaccompanied by a male relative.

Highly intelligent, multilingual, and a whiz at math, Anastas, before becoming a nun, taught many students not only how to think critically and solve problems correctly, but also how to be confident and excel.

Skilled in the nursing profession, she showed boundless empathy and energy as she provided loving service to others.

Sister Anastas was close to all people, especially the Palestinian Arab society. She cared deeply about the youth, the poor, the sick, and peace. Living in "the Land of the Cross" is never easy. She ached when people's rights were trampled upon, or when they were adversely affected, and continuously prayed for reconciliation in the Holy Land.

As witness of the Cross and bearer of the Resurrection, Sister Anastas struggled to sustain the presence, empowerment, and well-being of Christians in the Holy Land, while also benefitting the whole society. With its motto "So that they may be one," the visit of Pope Francis to the Holy Land meant a lot to her. She knew of the Pope's planned meeting with Ecumenical Patriarch Bartholomew I of Constantinople, which commemorated and reenergized the pledge to unity that Pope Paul VI and Patriarch Athenagoras I of Constantinople made when they met in Jerusalem in January 1964. As children growing up in Jerusalem, we deeply felt the impact of the historic visit as that occasion witnessed "let there be light"—the arrival of electricity to our Al-Thawri neighborhood of Jerusalem!

Sister Anastas sought the light in all she did. She took faith seriously and constantly put it into action. The Holy Family was her inspiration, as she loved and prayed for us—her own family—for the family of nuns with whom she lived and toiled for some thirty-seven years, and for the world. Determined and strong willed, she stood for what is right and was never shy at voicing her opinion about spiritual and secular issues.

The Blessed Virgin Mary, or *Theotókos* (Bearer of God) in the Orthodox Christian tradition, touched Sister Anastas's being and soul, and was, for her, a model of hope, love, sacrifice, and service. She took to heart what the Holy Bible, saints, and popes stated about loving the other, and put it into real, practical form. As Pope Francis explained, "To love God and neighbor is not something abstract, but profoundly concrete: It means seeing in every person the face of the Lord to be served, to serve him concretely. And you are, dear brothers and sisters, the face of Jesus."[179]

Sister Anastas passed away on Thursday, May 8, 2014. She rests in peace in the Roman Catholic Cemetery on Mount Zion, opposite Abu Tor and Al-Thawri, and in close proximity to the Room of the Cenacle,

Church of the Dormition of Mary, Cemetery of the Greek Orthodox Patriarchate where my father and grandparents are buried, and King David's Tomb. Her memory lives in me and in countless others. Her soul hovers in the Heavenly Jerusalem.

When I visited the cemetery in 2014, I could not help but be drawn to another grave, a stone's throw way from Sister Anastas's, almost fully covered with pebbles and small stones. It is that of Oskar Schindler ("Schindler's List"), with the German inscription, "The Unforgettable Lifesaver of 1200 Persecuted Jews," and the Hebrew inscription, "Righteous Among the Nations." Each of them, in her or his way, has brought comfort, meaning, and respect in our world. Their memories live in the hearts of multitudes.

Lucy

My third and younger sister, Lucia or Lucy, was only seven years old during the June 1967 War. Even at that tender age, she remembers much about its events and the pain of the grownups around her. Close to our grandmother, Futun, she encouraged her to be strong, as they "journeyed" away from home after being ordered by Israeli soldiers to do so on the morning of the war's third day, and then again when they returned home from Beit Sahour a few days later.

Lucy has also fond memories of the frequent visits to our grandfather Jani's house in Katamon, including the goldfish swimming around the water lilies in the small pond at the front of the house and the swing hanging from the huge fig tree in the backyard our grandfather installed for us. She enjoyed immensely, as I did, the chocolate pudding and *halawet el-sameed* (semolina pudding) our grandmother, Futun, prepared for us as she sat on *kursi el-qahwa* (little square wooden stool with woven rope; *karasi el-qahwa* [plural] are usually found in cafés) and told us stories of her youth with her rhythmic stirs of the small pot.

Lucy shared the bedroom with our grandmother and kept her company as she aged: "I had many a sleepless night," Lucy recalled. "Our grandmother had the habit to shout in her sleep, especially the last weeks of her life. She often called the name of her beloved mother."

In 1988, Lucy married Maurice Kattan, the son of Hanna and Emilie Kattan, who were among the few Arabs who remained in West Jerusalem. Maurice was able to buy back the different units in his parents' house in Abu Tor from the Jewish families who occupied them during the 1948 Arab-Israeli War. Tragically, he died four years later from a severe heart attack, leaving her with three young children and a whole lot of responsibility for a young woman in her early thirties.

Lucy's formative experiences and primary and secondary education at Saint Joseph School prepared her well for a life of service. The Eight Beatitudes Jesus gave in His Sermon on the Mount are never far from her heart and mind. Following her graduation from Bethlehem University, she worked initially for the Department of Social Services, part of the Community Services Administration in the Municipality of Jerusalem, and then at Saint Joseph Hospital. Later, she became the social worker at Saint Vincent de Paul, run by the Daughters of Charity of Saint Vincent de Paul, which serviced people of different ethnic and religious backgrounds and had a hospice, an orphanage, a nursery, a kindergarten, and a home for the elderly and infirm.

Conscientious and empathetic, Lucy went out of her way to assist those who are destitute or in crisis, by educating them about their rights and empowering them toward some form of satisfactory resolution. Sometimes, she was their voice when navigating the various public agencies and religious organizations, as well as the different cultural, legal, and linguistic paths of Jerusalem life. The toughest cases she handled dealt with drug addiction, extreme poverty, family violence, marital disputes, at-risk children, and religious intolerance. Yes, Jerusalem suffered and is suffering. While every hand matters, it takes many hands to uplift those in need.

In all, Lucy perseveres and does what is humanly possible, legal, and right. She is practical and knows that in addition to prayer, a good *sanad* (backing) goes a long way to effect change. When walking with her through Jerusalem, I cannot help but envy how people recognize her and thank her profusely for her many good deeds.

Brothers

Khamis

Born in 1947, one year before the first Arab-Israeli war, my eldest brother, Khamis, remembers nothing about the fighting and the internal displacement my family experienced. His earliest memories relate to his first day at Collège des Frères at age five, when he felt alone and had "to be on my own for the first time in my life; I had to depend on myself, no one else."

The Frères at that time consisted of two parts: a free school for poor students, and a tuition-based school for wealthy students or at least those who could afford to pay. The latter had "a boarding section with a large dormitory, a refectory, and a kitchen, for the use of which it charged student-boarders additional fees."[180] The caring De La Salle Brothers, Khamis recollects, fed him and the other poor students the leftover food from the wealthy students, including green beans and lentil soup. For dessert, they were often served orange peel. Although bitter, only the few would have known then that it contains the most beneficial and healthiest part of the entire orange!

Since early age, Khamis's focus has been on work—generating wealth and securing property. As a child and early adolescent, he filled most of his free time working at the goldsmith and jewelry store of George ᶜAkra and his sons, Khalil and Suheil. His business interests interrupted his studies at times, and he had to transfer schools, first to al-Ummah High School in Jerusalem and then to Collège des Frères in Bethlehem. At al-Ummah, he excelled in sports and was the volleyball captain. Among his classmates were the sons of the prominent Majali and Tuqan families in Jordan, and the ruling Sanussi family in Libya. Among his friends was Ayman Hazzaᶜ al-Majali, and the Jordanian officer driving Ayman and his older brother, Amjad, would often drop Khamis off at the Damascus Gate bus station before proceeding to Amman, where the Majali family lived.[181] At the Frères in Bethlehem, Khamis became the volleyball captain as well. But, his star rose when he rushed in 1966 to shut the external gate of the school from demonstrators against Jordanian rule in the West Bank, including East Jerusalem, thus ensuring the relative safety of the students and staff.

The post-June 1967 era provided Khamis with multiple opportunities, which he captured fully. He studied Hebrew at Ulpan Beit Ha'am, registered for business courses at the Hebrew University of Jerusalem, and then managed a cement and steel supply company owned by I. Lipman. He hired and fired employees, and sold tons of material, as a building boom transformed Jerusalem.

In few months, Khamis's comparative high income enabled him to buy a pickup truck and the neighbor's house. His attention then shifted to a sizeable piece of land my father bought on a hilltop in the southwest of Jerusalem, along with other members of the Greek Orthodox Club. Following the land's survey and subdivision, in addition to planting trees and fencing the lot, he built a two-bedroom house, with living room and bathroom. Khamis's excitement and sense of accomplishment came crashing down when the Israeli government expropriated the land and twelve-thousand-three-hundred other *dunams* (1 *dunam* equals 0.247 acre) in 1970, to build the settlement or neighborhood of Gilo, which it did starting in 1973. The house, the trees, and the fence—all were bulldozed in 1975. Minimal compensation for the land was offered, but none was accepted.

Khamis was unfazed. After leaving the Israeli cement and steel company, he rented a store in Bethlehem and started his own business, selling rattan furniture. Simultaneously, he entered into a business partnership to sell cement and steel. "In nine months," he commented, "I made more money than in seven years working as manager of the Israeli building supply company." He became a building contractor, renovating houses in Jerusalem's German Colony and Yemin Moshe, and helping to build a school in Rafidia, a neighborhood in the western section of the city of Nablus in the West Bank.

Being a resident of Jerusalem and driving his truck with yellow license plates through Palestinian areas, he became a target of violence. Youth showered his truck with stones but, fortunately, he escaped unscathed. He never returned to the Nablus area. Sometimes, when it rains, it pours. Khamis is sociable and likes to interact with people of all backgrounds. He befriended a Jewish girl, a new immigrant from Port Elizabeth in

South Africa. Her parents refused to meet him when they discovered he had Palestinian roots. It took three years for them to come around, but the relationship eventually dissolved. Being caught in the middle is often as dangerous or unpleasant as being on either side of the boundary.

Khamis looks at life from an apolitical perspective. For him, however, stealing of property by a government or a neighbor is equally wrong. The Eighth Commandment, "Thou shall not steal," is clear, and the laws should uphold this principle. The law of the jungle must be counteracted by effective laws that protect for all "life, liberty, and the pursuit of property."

Khamis visited the United States several times, eventually settling in Arizona. His business focus is alive and well. He keeps a watchful eye on his properties in Jerusalem and the U.S. The pursuit of property, in his mind, is the path to the pursuit of stability and happiness!

Michel

My second older brother, Michel, emphasized high culture and lifestyle. Composers like Wolfgang Amadeus Mozart and Pyotr Ilyich Tchaikovsky, singers like Nana Mouskouri and the beloved Lebanese singer, Nouhad Wadie^c Haddad, better known as Fairouz, and classical art and architecture appealed to his senses.

Like our father, he loved nature and knew the names of all kinds of vegetation. His boyhood hikes on Jerusalem's trails brought him in contact with the beautiful, pristine landscapes of the 1950s and 1960s, including the fig tree forest of Silwan, which has almost disappeared. He also frequented the dangerous and deserted spaces along no man's land and their wild flowers. He would bring home bunches of irises, white roses, red Crown Anemone, red Turban Buttercup, and red Sun-Eye Tulip, which our mother usually split into two small bouquets, the first as decoration for the Icon of the Anastasis (Resurrection), and the second as a centerpiece for our dining room table.

Michel was equally fascinated from early age by all kinds of drinks and foods. He would buy and let us taste a variety of cheeses, meats, pastries, and teas. He made delicious gravies and sauces. He was, and still is, a food connoisseur, and most of us thought that one day he will become a master chef or a famous wine critic.

As a child, Michel put his free time to good use. The summers between his ninth and eleventh birthdays were spent at the Greek Orthodox Patriarchal Printing Press, the same place where our father worked. He ran errands, fetched lunch for Father Modestos, the director, and made coffee for the employees on the same stove used to heat the glue for book binding. In subsequent summers, he worked at Marashelian Jewelers—owned by the Armenian family by the same name—near Jaffa Gate and learned basic jewelry making, in addition to some Armenian. He collected stamps, colorful stamps—a hobby that rubbed off on me as well.

As a schoolboy, Michel remembers a captivating encounter on a warm day in the Old City's Christian Quarter. With books in his hand, his eyes caught sight of Fairouz. He began walking alongside her through the cobblestone streets, the streets leading to the Church of the Holy Sepulchre. She finally sat down on a stone bench in the Church's square to catch her breath, to wipe off her brow. That is when he mustered enough courage to ask her gingerly: "Sing for us Fairouz, sing for us." She smiled, stood up, walked to the church entrance, and climbed up the worn stairs to what the Greek Orthodox call Golgotha or what the Latin/Roman Catholics call Calvary. Her prayers still echo: "Hope is ever-present. Hope is ever-present. Resurrection is the other side of crucifixion."

One of Michel's best friends in school was, and still is, Samir Jarallah, the son of Judge Nihad Jarallah, President of the West Bank Supreme Court. I joined them occasionally as they spent fun time, swimming and eating fruits of the earth at the family's plantations in Yaalo,[182] a Palestinian town located in the vicinity of the Latrun salient, in Jericho at the foot of the Mount of Temptations, and in Halhoul.[183] Michel also joined Ziad Salhab, another classmate and neighbor, on several visits to his family's vineyards in Halhoul. The grapes of Halhoul are incredibly tasty and among the world's best!

The last year in high school was instructive for Michel. Aside from solidifying his friendships with some of his classmates and teachers, he had a discouraging experience that ultimately uplifted his self-esteem and spirit. When he indicated his interest to take the General Certificate of Education (GCE) exam in Chemistry, his science teacher, Mr. Alex Hanania, who received fees per subject matter for the GCE, remarked in the presence of all the other teachers, "If only very few of my very best students do manage to pass, what makes you think you are ever going to pass?" He added, "Don't waste your parents' money; you will never pass." The results came out a few weeks later, and the one student to pass this specific exam not only at Collège des Frères, but also in all of Jerusalem, was Michel!

Michel had a tough time addressing the June 1967 War and its aftermath. The actual fighting, the separation from our family, facing death as he was delivering fresh bread to two elderly sisters during curfew—all left a deep mark on his psyche. As a free-spirited eighteen-year old, he took on the major responsibility of caring for me as we sought refuge and reunion with our family. Actually, he was *my* guardian angel.

In contrast to Khamis who focused on business, Michel pursued a different professional route. While he gave lessons in French to make extra cash, he considered going on a mission to Djibouti (which was the French Territory of the Afars and the Issas at the time), with Father Michel Sabbah (who later became Archbishop and Latin Patriarch of Jerusalem from 1987 to 2008) to teach French in addition to religious pursuits, but my parents objected due to the unsettling health and political conditions there. Instead, he worked at the YW (Young Women's Christian Association) in East Jerusalem, where he developed excellent friendships with tourists and United Nations personnel, some of whom frequented the YW. He learned Hebrew through occasional Israeli cultural osmosis. He preferred to study Greek and Spanish instead.

Following YW, Michel served as assistant to Father Maurice Benoit, OP, better known as Pierre Benoit, the Director of the École Biblique. It is an institute for advanced studies in archaeology and biblical science, with a universally acknowledged library on the subjects and with most of the instructors being members of the Académie des Arts et Belles-Lettres— the highest authority on the French language and literature. Michel also assisted the well-known archaeologist of the Dead Sea Scrolls, Father Roland Guérin de Vaux, OP. Through Fathers Benoit and de Vaux,

Michel met the top Israeli archeologists, like Yigael Yadin, who used the library or participated in talks and lectures. Knowing and working with these two special individuals of impeccable integrity left a lasting impact on Michel's attitude and appreciation of excellence, curiosity, and the true meaning of how one would be or behave as a real Christian.

A fringe benefit from that experience was the eye-opening culinary aspect of it. On special holidays, there would be a repast of ten to twelve course meals, matching food with wines with a succession from white, rose, red, and sweet as match for desserts. At the time, only the French knew how to have that type of tasting menus. Nowadays, many famous restaurants offer it.

Michel's love of nature and deep sense of justice made him critical of Israel's expansion in East Jerusalem and its environs. For him, the flowers, the trees, the open spaces were all sacrificed just to change the "facts on the ground." The tips of mountains were shaved "as if with chainsaws" to accommodate Israeli settlements. The housing congestion and the proliferation of television antennas and satellite dishes that overtook Jerusalem in successive years, moreover, made him claustrophobic. He felt the soul of the city was lost, not only the topography, but its unchanged charm through the millennia was eroded. Even the food, and many of the ingredients that he used to watch being hand-made, were gone and "never to return."

Michel left for the United States in the early 1970s, and soon thereafter joined the UN as an international civil servant. He retired 36 years later, having traveled the world and learned to manage in the six official languages of the UN, besides other languages and dialects. His love of nature has not subsided; during the past few years, he took no less than two-thousand photos of flowers from New York City's Central Park to Carl Czshurts Park, where Gracie Mansion is located (the official residence of NYC's Mayor). While strolling with his wife, he would point out to her songs of birds and unusual flowers and plants.

Jamil

My third older brother, Jamil, has excellent memories of the old days. He attended school at Collège des Frères and al-Ummah High School in

Jerusalem and Collège des Frères in Bethlehem and enjoyed interacting with teachers and students alike, including the sons of diplomats and United Nations personnel. He was active in programs and extracurricular activities, such as volunteering to show silent comedy films on a biweekly basis at the children's orphanage in Al-Izzariya. It was a three-to-four-hour commitment that involved traveling to location each other Saturday afternoon with a copy of the film to be shown, a projector, and a screen, and sitting through the screening. The laughs and smiles made it all worthwhile. It was a small act, but an impactful one on Jamil and the orphans.

As a teenager, Jamil marched to his tune, doing things his own way. The olive tree in the garden is our favorite; we watched it grow, we climbed it, we picked its fruits, and we took photos in front of it. One day, against parental warning, Jamil climbed the olive tree and chose one of its sturdy branches as his airplane cockpit. He rocked himself back and forth so forcefully for a few minutes, hoping for take-off, but soon found himself crash landing seven feet below—with the broken branch, the blood, and all. On another occasion, against parental warning again, he performed several somersaults, using as support the opposite middle rails of the two-sided door that leads from the living room to the dining room. On the third act, he fell and broke his right elbow. Stubbornness sometimes comes at a high cost.

Jamil is closer to Khamis in his attitude toward the changes that took place in Jerusalem after the June 1967 War, than Anastas and Michel. The war modified his view of authority and leadership. He lost confidence in politicians, the empty rhetoric of propagandists such as the Egyptian Ahmed Said of Sawt al-Arab, or Voice of the Arabs. The corruption of some in public life and undue influence of the connected, famous, and rich in Arab society turned him off. In a private conversation in the late 1970s with former Governor of Jerusalem Anwar Nusseibeh,[184] Mr. Nusseibeh asked Jamil not to misjudge what he sees: "We are what we are, and we have our traditions. Among us are the good and the bad, like any other people, but we are decent." While Jamil never denied Arab needs and potential, he was impressed, like many others, by the "ingenuity and progress" he witnessed in Israeli society.

If Jamil pursued his higher education, he would have become a historian or psychologist, as he has a keen eye for interpreting past and current events and gauging people's personalities. He has zero tolerance, as we all do, for corruption and deceit. For him, students who used to cheat on exams grow up to be dishonest. As he says, "they can hide their bad habits, they can control them, but they rarely change."

Spending most of his free time in Katamon, Jamil became close to our grandfather, Jani or Jamil, and our step-grandmother, Louisa. In time, he cared for them, as others in our family did, addressing most of their daily and health needs until their passing. Their remaining children, that is, our aunts and uncles, were residing in different parts of the world, including Australia, Germany, and Greece. On one occasion, walking home from Katamon, Jamil was stopped by a couple of Jewish men who urged him to join them for prayer. They were desperate to form a *minyan* (the quorum of ten Jewish adults needed for certain religious services in traditional Judaism). Although tempted, he thanked them for asking and continued on his way.

Throughout his adolescence and early adulthood, Jamil became saturated with Israeli and Western customs and spoke Hebrew fluently, in addition to Arabic, English, and French. For several years, he worked at an Israeli furniture store in the western side of Jerusalem and did well, developing the necessary knowledge and skills, which he then applied to the furniture business he built with our mother in Bethlehem. All came to a halt with the start of the First Intifada in 1987. Jamil left for California, where he still lives and runs his own furniture store.

Elias

My fourth and youngest brother, Elias, left Jerusalem in 1978 at age of 15. He joined me in the United States to pursue his high school education, as I was completing my higher education. He was too young to remember anything about Jordanian rule. What he remembers about the June 1967 War and how he was carried to safety by my eldest brother, Khamis, come mostly from the recollections of other family members.

Elias became close to our grandmother, Futun, who was homebound at the time he was entering his teens, and to our youngest sister, Lucy, who is four years his senior. From our grandmother, he learned much about her life story and how to cook, and from our sister, he learned to fend for himself as "the other grownups" were all busy pursuing their careers or education. Being the last of five brothers, he got used to hand-me down clothes, expertly retailored by our mother. Being the last of eight children, he embodies different traits of each of us: infinite kindness from Fatina, a volunteering spirit from Anastas, business acumen from Khamis and Jamil, drink and food appreciation from Michel, academic interests and conflict resolution from me, and dependability and helpfulness from Lucy.

School was fun for Elias, but not easy, as his teachers kept reminding him that they had us—four older brothers—in their classes, and he had to be a model student in terms of conduct, academics, and co-curricular activities. In mathematics, he stayed ahead of the curve through tutoring by Anastas. He excelled in English, which he learned not by memorizing the dictionary or reading major works of literature, but by watching what he calls "dust movies," or old Western cowboy films, mainly starring John Wayne, as in the *Stagecoach* (1939) or *The Cowboys* (1972). He also was mesmerized by watching, and re-watching, *James Bond* movies, starring, for example, Sean Connery or Roger Moore as Agent 007. Like several of us brothers, he was an altar boy, he volunteered at the food kiosk, he played soccer and volleyball, and he sang in the choir and chorus. All in all, he did exceedingly well to maintain the Sarsar good reputation!

Like all of us brothers and sisters, Elias had no real childhood. He had no choice but to grow up fast. His friendships were limited to his classmates at school; he rarely played with the neighborhood kids; "One day they play marbles with you," he stated, "and the next day they throw the marbles at you."

He sometimes accompanied Anastas, as I did on numerous occasions, on her religious and social outings. During one such outing at Emmaus—where Jesus Christ is believed to have appeared after His resurrection before two of his disciples, and the site of a Palestinian Arab village that was destroyed by Israel in 1967—he got the scare of his life. Another boy pushed him into a cactus shrub. Baptized with thorns, endless tears, and excruciating pain, it took Anastas hours, prayers, and salt to remove every thorn. It took weeks for the bruising to fully fade away. In another incident, this time riding behind Jamil on his bike, Elias brought his right ankle too close to the back-tire spokes, causing both of them to tumble and the blood to flow. Elias's ankle still bears the scar of that unfortunate day. In a third incident, Elias was making French fries and the hot oil splashed all over his left hand. The scars are no longer, but the memory of a third degree burn remains.

Elias's time was not all dramatic or all play. He began working the summer of his eighth birthday, initially at a wholesale canned food store near the Old City's Jaffa Gate, and then at the family's furniture store on the road to Bethlehem. "At age ten or eleven," he reminisced, "I was doing the work of a forty-year-old man." Moreover, Elias has a talent for fixing things. Whenever our old Phillips TV stopped working, or the picture on its screen went grainy or snowy, he would take it apart and reassemble it like new.

Elias has traveled back and forth between Arizona, where he lives and works in the furniture business, and Jerusalem. He, like all of us, wishes for peace and better relations between Palestinians and Israelis.

Letting My Young Life Speak

While it is hard to talk about oneself, I was told by several members of my family that my birth was a festive occasion, and that my childhood was a pleasant one. Upon arriving home from the hospital, both old and young were repeating out loud, "Saliba is here! Saliba is here!" All had a turn carrying me around. Being the number six child, I had more than a few hands taking care of me. My older sister, Anastas, was the closest, always ensuring my wellbeing.

By most standards, I was studious, attracted mostly to geography, history, languages, and literature. I remember walking back and forth, sometimes for hours, on our house's flat roof as I memorized hundreds of lines of Arabic and English poetry as well as the names of country capitals in preparation for school exams. That was a good exercise, physically and mentally!

As a teenager, I frequented the countless churches—Orthodox, Roman Catholic, and Protestant—that make Jerusalem their home. The two churches that deepened and still deepen my religious imagination the most are the Church of the Holy Sepulchre and the Church of Sitna Mariam near Gethsemane. I was inspired by icons, which are "windows into heaven," and became fascinated with Byzantine liturgical music.

On weekends or during vacation, in addition to volunteering, I sometimes used to go to the Old City and act as a guide for Western tourists, and I would be chased by the professional guides because I was taking their jobs away! In later years, I enjoyed taking my wife Hiyam and my daughters NoorEvelyn and Hania on guided tours of the Old City and her environs. With tourists all around us, I would raise my sun hat high in the air and shout out loud, "Bus number one," and we would all laugh.

My simple but mostly pleasant memories growing up relate to my family and my surroundings: Fatina's engagement party and her wedding ceremony, but also the sadness of her departure for Honduras; my father typesetting at the Greek Orthodox Patriarchal Printing Press; the *muezzin's* five daily calls to prayer and the sound of church bells; shopping with my grandmother in the Old City; Khamis picking pomegranates and *eskadenia* or loquat fruit from our garden's tall trees; watching the sun rise from behind the jasmine bush in bloom; playing with "sounounou," Michel's tortoise; wandering with Jamil close to no man's land; chasing fluffy, white bunnies with Lucy; holding tightly to Elias's hand at the crowded Church of the Holy Sepulchre; on Mother's Day, singing to my mother, "The field's wild birds sang to my mom. We came to be with her. What will the world be without her?"

My childhood memories came crashing down in June 1967. The Six-Day War and its effects shattered my inner innocence and my outer security, as they presented new openings toward a changed world, mainly the physical crossing of the border from East Jerusalem to West Jerusalem, and the psychological crossing of my identity from my Palestinian upbringing to my Greek-Russian heritage, and from Christian-Muslim culture to Jewish culture. In both crossings, and as I matured, I began to find countless similarities in difference and the value of cohering all I can, as best I can, so as to transcend boundaries. This I did by pursuing higher education in the United States, and continue to do through teaching as a professor of political science and Middle East studies and a philosophy of peace, dialogue, and engagement for a better tomorrow.

For me, peace is born by preparing for it. The responsibility for peace rests within all of us. Education for peace and dialogue are essential for disabling stereotypes, dispelling fear, and creating trust and compassion. A shared vision of peace, if supported by a strong political will and dedicated engagement by all parties concerned, can relieve society of the unknown and set the foundation for a sustainable culture of peace.

Dialogue is an essential element of the habits of peace. It is not about winning and losing. The intent of dialogue is not to reach agreement. Through storytelling and retelling, and the sharing of feelings, dialoguers connect through the heart, and then grow with "no walls, no checkpoints." New realities emerge. "You do not have to be wrong in order for me to be right!" By including all perspectives—not just some at the expense of others—dialoguers create trust, and then unprecedented learning, compassion, and creativity, to model a sustainable culture of peace. Dialogue can uncover not only liberation and empowerment, but conflicting narratives and emotional pain as well. Finally, as an equalizer of power, the dialogue process restores symmetry to relationships and enables participants to highlight similarities.

In this regard, our personal and collective responsibility is not to alter or compromise our identity to change our perspectives, but rather, as my Buddhist friend, Roshan Chaddha, believes, "to transcend our identity so that we can arrive at a common place with the other." Transcendence allows us to work through the paradox of despair on the ground and find hope in dialogue. Ultimately, we become advocates for many peoples, equally.

Israelis and Palestinians must improve the world they have made. It is in the best interest of their people and the common good. Israeli domination over millions of Palestinians is not defensible. The occupation must end. Likewise, complete Palestinian rule over the whole of historic Palestine is untenable and unacceptable. A single, democratic state in which Israeli Jews and Palestinians both ignore their ethno-national identities in favor of a combination of identities in a joint or bi-national state, while appealing to some, is not practical and will lead to a dead end. Israel and Palestine living alongside each other in peace and security, although not perfect or satisfactory to all, remains the most logical and practical. Neither Israelis nor Palestinians—both of whom exist in roughly equivalent numbers between the Jordan River and the Mediterranean Sea—are going to vanish from the land. Neither intends to abandon its identity or accept subjugation at the hands of the other.

Israeli and Palestinian leaders must think beyond their current conditions and the next election. They must seriously engage in negotiations to arrive at common interests. Only time will tell how they will work through their contending narratives and actualize a better world for their children and grandchildren. The sooner they start working on their *shared* destiny, the sooner they will reach a more hopeful future. The closer they get to the center, the more likely they are to succeed.

AFTERWORD
OUR SACRED TRUST

Where there is faith,
where there is resilience,
the future we seek is near.
Despair's depths are sharp;
the peak of hope is wondrous.
Rising from conflict and war,
the Holy City is eager to embrace all

of us—Jew and Arab; Israeli and Palestinian
Jewish, Christian, Muslim, and other.
Let empathy caress our negative minds,
Let the sun mend our broken hearts.
Let lively music enlighten our way.
The ascent awaits our steps;
the promise awaits to be kept.

A plant is well only when its roots are healthy. Healthy roots grow deep and strong when they are nourished by fertilized soil, sunshine, and water.

A house becomes a home when those living in it truly care about each other, and when they put their care and faith into action to serve others beyond themselves. Home is where charm, comfort, and warmth complement and supplement each other, with ever-growing goodness extending beyond it. It is where love and stewardship join hands.

A city becomes home when it has soul—when its spirit embraces its inhabitants and guests, ensuring their inclusion, involvement, and wellbeing. It becomes home when its inhabitants do right by others. It turns away from home when its inhabitants fight each other or engage in conflict.

Conflict, Loss, Pain

Over the millennia, Jerusalem has been less than a perfect home. In the 20th century alone, she changed hands from Ottoman to British, from British to Jordanian, and from Jordanian to Israeli—each with its own system of law and order. Ordinary families became subjected to surges of passion and bloodletting, often in the name of a "holy cause," namely nationalism, religion, territory. Borders—physical and psychological—went up and came down, with people making every effort to live within their confines and survive. Enemies were created—people demonized—because they happen to live on the other side of some imagined or real border.

At the start of the First World War, the brother of my grandfather Khamis was conscripted into the Ottoman army and never returned home. During the 1936-1939 Civil War, along with millions of other inhabitants, my family went through the hardest times. In the 1948 and 1967 wars, my family felt both inordinate fear and internal displacement, which were miniscule compared to the experiences of others—many of whom lost their lives, were wounded, were stranded in refugee camps, or ended up in the diaspora. The first and second Palestinian intifadas against the Israeli occupation caused economic, financial, and freedom costs, aside from the destruction of life and property.

As a child, I could hardly imagine that my family would be caught up in this trap. We were prisoners of our peculiar environment. As an adult, I am torn between the light of childhood and the dark deeds that still haunt Jerusalem.

Why must the innocent undergo the ritual of insecurity and battle? Why all the blood and self-deluding sacrifice? Why must the sacraments of bread and wine be consumed before people come to their senses? Why does the city of holy men and women, of saints, suddenly change into warring madness?

Answers rest mostly with those in authority who are ultimately responsible for war, peace, security, and for life and death decisions. What they say and do can cause catastrophe in the form of creating enemies, no man's land, refugees, and dispossession, or they can bring about peace, justice, and prosperity.

Habits of Peace

Jews, Christians, and Muslims—Israelis, Palestinians, and others—continue to suffer terribly in Jerusalem and her environs. Their lives, property, and future are continually being threatened. Many have died or have been maimed in Jerusalem's name. Their descendants carry negative memories and deep scars for generations.

We—the ordinary people—need to remain vigilant and not fall prey to the temptations of aggrandizement and power. Our responsibility is to avoid getting caught in a self-made cage of aggression and war. We must realize that what inhibits something from happening can allow it to happen. What separates can bind. What kills can be transformed to inspire life. Borders, refugees, and enemies—all boundary-bound—can be regenerated: borders into human bridges and gardens, refugees into settled peoples, and enemies into friends. Worldviews that propel human experience toward war can equally make it meaningful for social justice and economic wellbeing. Out of a universe of ambiguity, contradictions, and hopelessness can arise a culture of peace. In this universe, killing without guilt and slaughtering without shame will no longer be acceptable. People will stop being hurdles on the way; rather, they will become the way.

Instead of projecting upon the enemy a face of cruelty and hatred, we need to project what is in us and what we desire for ourselves. The hostile imagination must diminish, if the meeting of minds is to convene. The icon of the enemy must evolve into a three-dimensional image of a friend, if the seeds of peace are to bloom. It is then that the border itself will stop being an end in itself. It evolves into becoming a bridge to better possibilities.

Jerusalemites are entitled to have a roof over their head. They have to be able to walk out of their doors and look about their plots, however large or small, and say: "This is ours." They have to be able to touch the earth with their forehead, to kneel or stand, or to rock back and forth. They have to be able to call their children and say: "When we have gone out, or we have gone up, or we have been set in the earth, this land shall be yours." It is important for each of them to enjoy the garden's flowers—smell a rose here and there—because the garden of life belongs to all.

As I reflect on my family's story and the evolution of Jerusalem and Al-Thawri, as I listen to my life, and as I ponder our individual and collective responsibilities, I cannot help but think that, irrespective of our loyalties and partisan views, our voice and our touch must indicate that chauvinism, exclusion, and intolerance are harmful and run counter to Jerusalem's spirit, even though they might benefit the radical few. Extremism and violence must stop—and stop *now*. Those who willfully use their direct or indirect power to aggress against others or twist ideas to demonize "the other" have veered away from the sacred trust.

Jerusalem and Us: A Symbiotic Relationship

My family's sense of belonging and gratefulness to Jerusalem emanates from our close ties and lived experiences in the Holy City. Jerusalem's joys and heartaches are our joys and heartaches.

My life—my identity—would not be the same without Jerusalem: family roots; grandparents; parents; siblings; other family members; friends; neighbors; faith, spiritual fathers and mothers; holy sites; the Old City sights, scents, and sounds; mentors and educational institutions; acts of kindness across divides and amidst conflict, destitution, and pain—all combine to strengthen my attachments and sustenance.

Abu Tor/Al-Thawri, where I grew up and played, has a tremendous impact on who I am and how I view reality. It is where my family has lived since 1942. Regardless of its challenges, it is where I feel connected. It is where I lived the border, but took the opportunity to overcome it. No matter where my parents and siblings have travelled and how long they have stayed away from home, they feel comfortable at home in Jerusalem.

As a family, we sometimes wonder what would have become of our orphaned father, Ivan (later renamed Hanna and then George), if it were not for the kindness of his caretaker, Tatiana, and strangers who made him their own (the Zananiri and Sarsar families, respectively?). What would have happened to our mother, Evelyn, when her own mother, Anastasia, died, if it were not for the love of her maternal grandmother, Mariam, and her aunts, Futun and Julia? Would Futun have been able to care for her dying husband, Khamis, and provide a home for her mother, Mariam, her adoptive son, George, and her niece, Evelyn, if it were not for the generosity and hospitality of Signe Ekblad, the headmistress of the Swedish School? Would our mother, suffering from amalgam poisoning during the internal displacement of 1948, have survived without the medical care of Dr. Adamany, the good dentist, and George Haddad, the male staff nurse with the Arab Legion? Would we, as children, have had a comfortable life—when we were truly poor—if it were not for the care and love of our parents and grandmother, as well as the care and generosity of our godparents, Mary and Nasser Mukhar? Would Michel and I have found our way to safety during the June 1967 War if it were not for the goodness of Father Theodosios and the Salfiti family? Would Michel be alive if it were not for the reasonable Israeli officer intervening in time to prevent the rash Israeli soldier from shooting him during the curfew hours of a June 1967 day? Would our family members have become permanent refugees if the Abu Sᶜdah family did not host them at their home in Beit Sahour?

Without doubt, there was, and *is*, something miraculous at work. My family's roots, associated with the city of Jerusalem for over a century and a half, would not have been able to grow well without the selfless acts of others and without the faith, hope, and resilience of family members. At our time of need, caring hands reached out to us with love. We reciprocated with faithful service and prayers. In poverty, we appreciated faith, not as a sedative but out of thankfulness for the little we had and hope for better times. In conflict and war, we felt the importance of faith, not out of fear but out of the will to survive and hope for peace.

Our experience—our story—is not the exception. Countless other families have suffered, but also benefited, from the goodness of others.

FAMILY PHOTOS
All photographs are the property of the Sarsar family

Mother's paternal grandfather
George Damianou Korfiatis

Left to right: Mariam Zahra Qaraʿa, Mother's maternal grandmother and her three daughters:
Anastasia, front, sitting; Julia, standing; and Futun, left, sitting

Framed photo of Khamis Salim Abdo Sarsar,
Father's adoptive father

Framed photo of Futun Hanna Qara'a Sarsar,
Father's adoptive mother and Mother's aunt

Mother's parents Anastasia Hanna Qara‛a Korfiatis and
Jani "Jamil" Korfiatis, 1925

Little Evelyn Korfiatis in kindergarten at the Swedish School, c. 1931
Second row, second from left, with
Headmistress Signe Ekblad sitting down in back row

Front, sitting: Evelyn's grandmother Mariam Zahra Qara'a
Back row, left to right: George, Futun, and Evelyn

George Sarsar and Evelyn Korfiatis Sarsar's Wedding Day
June 7, 1942, Swedish School, Jerusalem
Left to right: Futun Hanna Qara ͨa Sarsar, best man Nasser Mukhar, George Sarsar, Evelyn Korfiatis Sarsar, bridesmaid Mary Mukhar, and Mariam Zahara Qara ͨa, Futun's mother and Evelyn's grandmother

Evelyn Korfiatis Sarsar and George Sarsar
Wedding Day, June 7, 1942

Father George Sarsar

Mother Evelyn Korfiatis Sarsar

Front row, left to right: Fatina, Anastas, Michel, Jamil, Khamis
Back row, left to right: father George carrying Saliba, mother Evelyn, c. 1958

The Sarsar children, c. 1959
Front row, left to right: Michel, Saliba, Jamil
Back row, left to right: Anastas, Fatina, Khamis

Front row, left to right: Jamil, Lucy on mother's lap, Saliba
Second row, left to right: mother Evelyn, Michel, c. 1961

Left to right: grandmother Futun, mother Evelyn, Saliba,
Fatina, Khamis, father George, Jamil, and Anastas

Fatina

Mother Evelyn and Fatina: Engagement Day

High School Graduation, College de Terre-Sainte,
Soeurs de St. Joseph, Jerusalem, May 12, 1974.
Left to right: Jamil, Saliba, the graduate,
mother Evelyn, grandmother Futun,
sister Anastas, father George, Khamis

Left to right: Sisters Anastas and Lucy

Left to right: Jamil, Khamis, Saliba, Elias

Hiyam and Saliba's Wedding Day, July 5, 1996, Mar Elias, Jerusalem. Left to right: father George, mother Evelyn, Lucy and her son Yuhanna, Hiyam, Saliba and Lucy's daughter Christine, Elias and Lucy's daughter Emily, and Sister Anastas

Left to right: Saliba and Michel

Left to right: Saliba and Michel

Sister Anastas

Left to right: Lucy, Saliba,
Mother Evelyn, Elias, May 2014

Fatina

Saliba, parents' home in Al-Thawri
The Old City of Jerusalem and
her environs in the background

ENDNOTES

Preface: A Living Mosaic

1. Meron Benvenisti, *Jerusalem: The Torn City* (Jerusalem: Isratypeset Ltd., 1976).
2. Amos Elon, *Jerusalem: City of Mirrors* (London: Fontana, 1989).
3. Meron Benvenisti, *City of Stone: The Hidden History of Jerusalem* (Oakland, CA: University of California Press, 1998).
4. Menachem Klein, *Jerusalem: The Contested City* (New York: New York University Press, 2001).
5. Bernard Wasserstein, *Divided Jerusalem: The Struggle for the Holy City*, 2nd Ed. (New Haven and London: Yale Nota Bene, 2002).
6. Philip Misselwitz and Tim Rieniets, *City of Collision: Jerusalem and the Principles of Conflict Urbanism* (Berlin: Birkhäuser Architecture, 2006).
7. Michael Dumper, *Jerusalem Unbounded: Biography, History & the Future of the Holy City* (New York: Columbia University Press, 2014).
8. Lena Jayyusi, ed., *Jerusalem Interrupted: Modernity and Colonial Transformation, 1917-Present* (Northampton, MA: Olive Branch Press, 2015).
9. Paola Caridi, *Jerusalem without God: Portrait of a Cruel City* (Cairo: The American University in Cairo Press, 2017).
10. Karen Armstrong, *Jerusalem: One City, Three Faiths* (New York: Ballantine, 1996), xvi.
11. Ibid.
12. David Rosen, "The Spiritual Significance of Jerusalem in Judaism," http://www.rabbidavidrosen.net/Articles/
13. Michel Sabbah, with Drew Christiansen and Saliba Sarsar, eds. *Faithful Witness: On Reconciliation and Peace in the Holy Land* (Hyde Park, NY: New City Press, 2009), 102.
14. Jayson Casper, "Holy Sepulchre will Reopen After Jerusalem Suspends Church Tax Grab," *Christianity Today* (February 27, 2018), http://www.christianitytoday.com/news/2018/february/holy-sepulchre-reopen-jerusalem-suspend-church-tax-property.html.
15. Ziad Abu-Amr, "The Significance of Jerusalem: A Muslim Perspective," *Palestine-Israel Journal* 2, 2 (1995), http://www.pij.org/details.php?id-646.

16　William Dalrymple, *From the Holy Mountain: A Journey Among the Christians of the Middle East* (New York: Henry Holt and Co., 1997), 310.
17　See Custodia Terrae Sanctae, "Opening of Church of the Holy Sepulchre," http://www.sepulchre.custodia.org/default.asp?id=4127.
18　An important corrective is the dual-narrative approach that allows Jewish Israelis and Palestinians to learn the history of the other party in the conflict so as to give up demonizing the "other." See Sami ʿAdwan, Dan Bar-On, and Eyal Naveh, eds. PRIME Peace Research Institute in the Middle East. *Side By Side: Parallel Histories of Israel-Palestine* (New York: The New Press, 2012).
19　Saliba Sarsar, "Jerusalem: Between the Local and Global," *Alternatives: Turkish Journal of International Relations* 1, 4 (Winter 2002): 54.
20　Bernard Wasserstein, *Divided Jerusalem*, ibid., x.
21　Ibid.
22　Ibid., xi.
23　Menachem Klein, *Lives in Common: Arabs and Jews in Jerusalem, Jaffa and Hebron* (New York: Oxford University Press, 2014).
24　Jalal al-Din Rumi. *The Essential Rumi*, translated by Coleman Barks and John Moyne (San Francisco: HarperOne, 2004), 16.

1. War, 1967

25　Tom Segev. *1967: Israel, the War and the Year that Transformed the Middle East* (London: Abacus, 2008).
26　The Six-Day War can be called the Two-and-a-Half-Day War in Jerusalem as it started on Monday morning, June 5, 1967, and ended on Wednesday afternoon, June 7, 1967.
27　The Cambon Declaration, a letter written by Jules Cambon, the Secretary General of Foreign Affairs in France, to Nahum Sokolow, at the time head of the political wing of the World Zionist Organization in London, reads in part: "You were good enough to present the project to which you are devoting your efforts, which has for its object the development of Jewish colonization in Palestine. You consider that, circumstances permitting, and the independence of the Holy Places being safeguarded on the other hand, it would be a deed of justice and of reparation to assist, by the protection of the Allied Powers, in the renaissance of the Jewish nationality in that Land from which the people of Israel were exiled so many centuries ago. The French Government…can but feel sympathy for your cause, the triumph of which is bound up with that of the Allies…"
28　The Balfour Declaration, a letter written by Arthur James Balfour, the Foreign Secretary of the United Kingdom, to Walter Rothschild of the British Jewish community, reads: "His Majesty's Government view with

favor the establishment in Palestine of a national home for the Jewish people, and will use their best endeavors to facilitate the achievement of this object, it being clearly understood that nothing shall be done which may prejudice the civil and religious rights of non-Jewish communities in Palestine or the rights and political status enjoyed by Jews in any other country."

29 An earlier version of the way my family and I experienced the June 1967 War appeared in my 1999 article. See Saliba Sarsar, "Memories of Al-Thori," *The Jerusalem Quarterly File*, 5 (Summer 1999): 31-40, http://www.palestine-studies.org/sites/default/files/jq-articles/5_Memories_1.pdf.

30 This line, drawn in green on the map, demarcated a temporary border between Jordan and Israel. It was a result of negotiations that ended the 1948 Arab-Israeli War, and was enshrined in the 1949 Armistice Agreement.

31 The United Nations Emergency Force was created by the United Nations General Assembly in November 1956 and with the Egyptian government's consent. Its key mission was to end the Suez Crisis and deploy troops along the Egyptian-Israeli border for the purpose of observation, mainly to prevent the remilitarization of the Sinai Peninsula.

32 The Strait of Tiran separates the Gulf of Aqaba from the Red Sea. By closing it, Abdel-Nasser prevented all shipping to and from Israel's Port of Eilat. Most affected at that time was Israel's access to the Red Sea, especially its oil importation from Iran.

33 The Nakba denotes the tragedy that impacted Palestinian Arabs from late December 1947 to early 1949. In addition to the war's dead and wounded, over 700,000 fled or were ejected from their homes in historic Palestine and prevented from returning to them after the war ended.

34 Sari Nusseibeh, with Anthony David, *Once Upon A Country: A Palestinian Life* (New York: Farrar, Straus and Girouz, 2007), 88.

35 Simon Sebag Montefiore, *Jerusalem: The Biography* (New York: Vintage Books, 2011), 512.

36 "King Hussein of Jordan," *The Telegraph*, February 8, 1999, http://www.telegraph.co.uk/news/obituaries/royalty-obituaries/7136625/King-Hussein-of-Jordan.html.

37 Sari Nusseibeh, with Anthony David, *Once Upon A Country*, ibid., 93.

38 Our father told us that Father Theodosios even saved the life of Prince Hussein of Jordan sixteen years earlier. He is Theodosios Makkos who was born in Smyrna, present-day Turkey, on July 11, 1913. Orphaned at an early age, he was raised by his devout grandmother and aunt who probably visited the Holy Land as pilgrims and planted in young Theodosios' spirit the love they have for Jesus Christ and the Church. At age 13, he left for

Jerusalem where he stayed for the rest of his life, passing away in 1991. On July 20, 1951, when King Abdullah of Jordan was visiting the Al-Aqsa Mosque in Jerusalem to eulogize Lebanon's Prime Minister Riad al-Solh, who was assassinated in Amman three days earlier, an assassin's bullet ended his life as well. His 15-year old grandson Prince Hussein ibn Talal by his side was also shot but a medal he wore that day deflected the bullet, thus saving his life. Since no one knew the details of the assassination plot at that immediate time, Father Theodosios placed Prince Hussein under his cassock, or soutane, and headed to the Greek Orthodox Patriarchate, a distance of 1.24 miles (2 km), where he hid him until an official Jordanian delegation came to escort the Prince safely back to Amman. Father Theodosios and Prince Hussein (who became King of Jordan from 1953 to 1999) developed a close friendship and occasionally visited each other. This story is retold by Rev. George C. Papademetriou who visited with Father Theodosios in January 1986. Father Theodosios also told of how whenever King Hussein "greeted him as a sign of respect the king opened his palm for him to kiss, whereas the other people kissed the back of his hand." George C. Papademetriou, "An Orthodox Christian Monk Saved the Life of a Muslim Prince", *Hellenic News of America*, February 4, 2005, https://groups.yahoo.com/neo/groups/OrthodoxNews/conversations/topics/2517.

39   "The Battle for Abu Tor," The Jerusalem Brigade, Ammunition Hill National Memorial Site, www.g-h.or.il/en/about/ammunition-hill-battle/jerusalem-division.

40   Abraham Rabinovich, *The Battle for Jerusalem: June 5-7, 1967* (Philadelphia, PA: The Jewish Publication Society of America), 358.

41   Don Nissenbaum, *A Street Divided: Stories from Jerusalem's Alley of God* (New York: St. Martin's Press, 2015), 62.

42   Ibid.

43   Rabinovich, *The Battle for Jerusalem: June 5-7, 1967*, 370.

44   Ein Rogel is associated with Job's Well or Bir Ayyūb, located at the intersection of the Hinnom Valley and the Kidron Valley near Siloam or Silwan outside the Old City of Jerusalem.

45   Meron Benvenisti, *Conflicts and Contradictions* (New York: Villard Books, 1986), 107.

46   This decision was reversed following huge popular demonstrations and a vote of confidence by the Egyptian National Assembly.

2. Post-War Echoes

47   David Ben-Gurion was Israel's key founder and first Prime Minister.

48 Betty Dagher Majaj, *A War Without Chocolate: One Woman's Journey Through Two Nations, Three Wars, and Four Children* (Middletown, DE: np, 2015), 169.

49 For a discussion of several of these events, see Meron Benvenisti, *Jerusalem: The Torn City*, ibid., 86-88.

50 Tom Abowd, "The Moroccan Quarter: A History of the Present," *Journal of Palestine Studies* 7 (2000): http://www.palestine-studies.org/jq/fulltext/78159.

51 Meron Benvenisti, *City of Stone: The Hidden History of Jerusalem*, ibid., 82.

52 Usama Halabi, "The Legal Status of Palestinians in Jerusalem," *Palestine-Israel Journal* 4, 1 (1997): www.pij.org/details.php?id=505.

53 See, for instance, Hazem Zaki Nusseibeh, *Palestine and the United Nations* (London: Quartet Books, 1981), 91-103.

54 Hala Sakakini, *Jerusalem and I: A Personal Record* (Amman, Jordan: Economic Press Co., 1990), xiv.

55 The song, sponsored by the Jerusalem Municipality was written by the leading Israeli lyricist and musician Naomi Shemer. For translations of the song, see http://www.jerusalemofgold.co.il/ translations.html.

56 Fairuz, "Zahrat El-Mada'en," lyricstranslate.com/en/node/77817.

57 Betty Dagher Majaj, *A War Without Chocolate*, ibid., 170-171.

58 Collège des Frères is a Catholic institution of education founded by the La Salle Brothers in 1876. The school provides outstanding scientific, educational, spiritual, and cultural programs" and extracurricular activities "designed to help develop the students' personality, social capabilities, and skills." Moreover, it "aspires at nurturing creative and responsible individuals, armed with civilized and human values based on freedom, love, tolerance, and respect for others". For details, see http://www.cdf.edu.ps/en/?page_id=177.

59 Khartoum Resolutions, September 1967, *Middle East Web*, http://www.mideastweb.org/khartoum.htm.

60 United Nations Security Council, "Resolution 242 of 22 November 1967," https://unispal.un.org/DPA/DPR/unispal.nsf/0/7D35E1F729DF491C85256EE700686136.

3. Family Roots

61 These dates are in the Gregorian calendar, which correspond to February 1917 and October 1917 in the Julian calendar that was in use in Russia at the time.

62 Kent Sole and Paul Gilbert, "The Fate of the Romanovs: The Survivors," www.angelfire.com/pa/imperialRussian/royalty/russia/ survivor.html.

63 The Crimean War was caused by superpower competition, mainly the United Kingdom and France preventing Czarist Russia from gaining a foothold in the Ottoman Empire, and set off by disagreement over the rights of Christian communities in the Holy Land.

64 Samih K. Farsoun and Naseer H. Aruri, *Palestine and the Palestinians: A Social and Political History*. 2nd ed., (Boulder, CO: Westview Press, 2006), 35-44.

65 Russian Jews also came in the thousands, but for different reasons. Their pilgrimage to Jerusalem was permanent. Martin Gilbert writes, they sought "an escape from the physical persecution of Tsardom,…the threat of twenty-five years' military service, and the violence of the anti-Jewish pogroms of the early 1880s, as well as the fulfillment of their spiritual longings." Martin Gilbert, *Jerusalem: Rebirth of a City* (New York: Elisabeth Sifton Books, Viking, 1985), xii.

66 Samih K. Farsoun and Naseer H. Aruri, *Palestine and the Palestinians: A Social and Political History*, ibid., 39.

67 The monotheistic faiths of Judaism, Christianity, and Islam view Jerusalem as the center of the world. While Jews include the whole city, Christians, at least the Greek Orthodox among them, mark the center by a stone bowl on the floor of the Catholicon in the Church of the Holy Sepulchre and Muslims locate it at the Dome of the Rock. One medieval Christian map showed Jerusalem at the heart of the three known continents of Africa, Asia, and Europe.

68 See Russian Ecclesiastical Mission in Jerusalem, "Mission's History," http://www.jerusalem-mission.org/history.html.

69 Joseph B. Glass and Ruth Kark, *Sephardi Entrepreneurs in Jerusalem: The Valero Family, 1800-1948* (Jerusalem: Gefen Publishing House Ltd., 2007), 116-118.

70 See Wasif Jawhariyyeh in Salim Tamari and Issam Nassar, eds., *The Storyteller of Jerusalem: The Life and Times of Wasif Jawhariyyeh, 1904-1948* (Northampton, MA: Olive Branch Press, Interlink Publishing Group, Inc., 2014), 81.

71 Stephen Graham, *With the Russian Pilgrims to Jerusalem* (London: Macmillan and Co., Limited, 1914), 153-154.

72 Salim Tamari, *Year of the Locust: A Soldier's Diary and the Erasure of Palestine's Ottoman Past* (Berkeley: University of California Press, 2011) and Stefani Wichhart, "The 1915 Locust Plague in Palestine," *Jerusalem Quarterly* 56 & 57 (2013): 29-39.

73 Amy Dockser Marcus, *Jerusalem 1913: The Origins of the Arab-Israeli Conflict*. New York: Viking, 2007), 142.

74 For an elaboration on the believers' religious fervor, see Wasif Jawhariyyeh in Salim Tamari and Issam Nassar, eds., *The Storyteller of Jerusalem: The Life and Times of Wasif Jawhariyyeh, 1904-1948*, ibid., 45-46.

75 Infectious diseases, such as typhus, recurrent fever, dysentery, and malaria, were a serious problem during the First World War. Typhus outbreaks among civilians occurre in Jerusalem, Aleppo, Damascus, and Beirut. See Melanie Schulze-Tanielian, "Disease and Public Health: Ottoman Empire/Middle East," *International Encyclopedia of the First World War*. http://www.academic.edu/8688608/ Disease_and_Public-Health_in_ the_Ottoman_Empire_during_WWI.

76 Communal boundaries in the Old City are a creation of the British Mandate. As Salim Tamari explains in his introduction to Wasif Jawhariyyeh's memoirs, "The British demarcated new boundaries between the city's populations to preserve equilibrium and create a modern sectarian balance among the four ancient communities. This balance preserved the status quo in the administration of the holy sites, an arrangement carefully negotiated during the late Ottoman period, and elaborated and codified in the early mandate rule over the city". Salim Tamari, "Introductions: I. Wasif Jawhariyyeh's Jerusalem" in Salim Tamari and Issam Nassar, eds., *The Storyteller of Jerusalem: The Life and Times of Wasif Jawhariyyeh, 1904-1948*, ibid., XVIII.

77 The 1908 Young Turk Revolution introduced major reforms that consisted of reviving the Ottoman Constitution, among others. This made military service compulsory for all Ottoman subjects, including Christian Arabs. See Martin Gilbert, *Jerusalem in the Twentieth Century* (New York: John Wiley & Sons, Inc., 1996), 17-18.

78 Issa J. Boullata, *The Bells of Memory: A Palestinian Boyhood in Jerusalem* (Westmount, Quebec: Linda Leith Publishing, 2014), 57.

79 Yousef and Najeeb ᶜAbdo, half-brothers of Sultaneh ᶜAbdo Sakakini, are cousins of Khamis Salim ᶜAbdo Sarsar, and Hala, Dumia, and Sari Sakakini, the children of Khalil and Sultaneh Sakakini are distant cousins of the Sarsar Family.

80 See Itamar Katz & Ruth Kark, "The Church and Landed Property: The Greek Orthodox Patriarchate of Jerusalem," *Middle Eastern Studies* 43, 3 (May 2007): 383-408. The church owns over two-thirds of the land and a sizeable portion of the property in the Old City. "In West Jerusalem alone, the Knesset [Israeli Parliament], the Supreme Court, the Israel Museum, and official residences of the president and prime minister all sit on land owned by the Greek Orthodox Church". See Donna Rosenthal, *The Israelis* (New York: Free Press, 2003), 309.

81 Bertha Spafford Vester is the daughter of Horatio and Anna Spafford. In 1881, the Spaffords arrived in Jerusalem and settled in the Old City. In

time, they developed the American Colony and were of great assistance to all those in need. The First World War proved most challenging as famine, plague, and injury devastated the people. The Spaffords met the challenge by operating a soup kitchen, hospitals for the wounded, and an embroidery industry that "sustained about 300 women whose husbands, fathers, and brothers were in the army of forced labor corps." See the American Colony in Jerusalem Exhibition. Wartime Aid. www.loc.gov/exhibits/ americancolony/amcolony-aid.html. Bertha continued to play a leading role by creating a baby home that became a children's hospital and then a children's medical center decades later, with outreach programs in the West Bank.

82 Among the cities damaged in Mandated Palestine were Jericho, Jerusalem, Hebron, Nablus, Lydda, Ramle, and Tiberias. In Transjordan, the cities included Amman and Es-Salt.

83 The word Katamon originates from the Greek kata tōi monastēriōi ("under the monastery"), and it believed that Simeon who recognized Jesus as the promised Messiah lived there. In the latter part of the 19th century, the Greek Orthodox Church built a church and a residence for the Patriarch, which he used as a summer home. Since 1948, Katamon has been a Jewish neighborhood. However, between 1914 and 1948, Arab families, Christian and Muslim, in addition to Greeks, Armenians, and Russians, made Katamon their home. See Hala Sakakini's book of reminiscences, *Jerusalem and I, A Personal Record*, ibid., for the attached drawing of the Katamon neighborhood, which she did from memory and which details the names and locations of families, churches, grocery stores, tailors, hotels, and bus routes at that time.

84 Anastasia and Jani traveled by horse-drawn carriage to Katamon to inspect the location near Saint Simeon and then used the 100 dinars she saved from her embroidery work to buy the land.

4. Parents' Wedding

85 Kimberly Katz, translator, annotator, introducer, *A Young Palestinian's Diary, 1941-1945: The Life of Sami ʿAmer* (Austin: University of Texas Press, 2009), 5.

86 See Wasif Jawhariyyeh in Salim Tamari and Issam Nassar, eds., *The Storyteller of Jerusalem: The Life and Times of Wasif Jawhariyyeh, 1904-1948*, ibid., 202. Jawharriyeh's casualty figures are higher than other sources. According to Kimberly Katz, ibid., those killed numbered 133 Jews and at least 116 Arabs.

87   Avraham Sella, "The 'Walling Wall' Riots (1929) as a Watershed in the Palestine Conflict," *The Muslim World*, LXXXIV, 1-2 (January-April 1994): 60.
88   In September 1929, the British dispatched the (Sir Walter) Shaw Commission. Its report, issued in March 1930, cited Arab fears of persistent Jewish immigration and land purchases as the main cause. This was followed by the creation of the (Sir John) Hope Simpson Enquiry in May 1930, which focused on the issues of immigration, land settlement, and development. Its report, dated October 1, 1930, recommended limiting Jewish immigration based on the economic absorptive capacity of Palestine. The same day, the Passfield White Paper was issued, also restricting Jewish immigration.
89   Inger Marie Okkenhaug, "Signe Ekblad and the Swedish School in Jerusalem 1922-1948". *Swedish Missiological Themes* 94, 2 (2006), E1466. blogspot.com/2012/05/signe-ekblad-and-swedish-school-in.html.
90   The British established the (William) Peel Commission to examine the reasons for the strife, which it did in November 1936. In July 1937, the commission presented partition as the solution to the Arab-Jewish Conflict. The Arab leadership, as represented by both the Arab Higher Committee and the National Defense Party, opposed the recommendation on the grounds that it violated the rights of the Arab population. The (Sir John) Woodhead Commission in 1938 gave further consideration to the Peel Commission proposal and found it to be impractical given the administrative, financial, and political obstacles in the way of partition. In 1939, the British issued a White Paper that rejected partition and the establishment of a Jewish state. The latter could only happen with Arab support. It opted instead for the creation of a Jewish national home in an independent Palestinian state within 10 years. It also restricted Jewish immigration into Palestine and the Jewish ability to buy Arab land.
91   Samih K. Farsoun and Naseer H. Aruri, *Palestine and the Palestinians: A Social and Political History*, ibid., 89.
92   Michael Gasper, "The Making of the Modern Middle East," in Ellen Lust, ed., *The Middle East*. 13th ed. (Thousand Oaks, CA: CQ Press, 2014), 36.
93   Matthew Hughes, "From Law and Order to Pacification: Britain's Suppression of the Arab Revolt in Palestine, 1936-39." *Journal of Palestine Studies*, XXXIX, 2 (Winter 2010): 6-22.
94   Baruch Kimmerling and Joel S. Migdal, *Palestinians: The Making of a People* (New York: Free Press, 1993), 123.
95   Matthew Hughes, "The Banality of Brutality: British Armed Forces and the Repression of the Arab Revolt in Palestine, 1936-39." *English Historical Review*, CXXIV, 507 (2009): 313-354.

96   Shlomo Ben-Ami, *Scars of War, Wounds of Peace: The Israeli-Arab Tragedy* (New York: Oxford University Press, 2006), 7.

97   For a short biography of Prince Ras Kassa, see Solomon Kibriye, "Ras Kassa Hailu," https://www.flickr.com/photos/71322788@N07/ 4625173691.

98   As the Palestinian Arab Revolt was extinguished, the Second World War was igniting. While many Jews and some Palestinians fought on the side of the Allies, Jerusalem's Grand Mufti Mohammed Amin al-Husseini assisted Fascist Italy and Nazi Germany. During his meeting with Adolf Hitler in 1941, he asked for support with Arab independence and with opposition to a Jewish national home in Palestine. See Taysir Jbara, *Palestinian Leader Hajj Amin Al-Husayni Mufti of Jerusalem* (Princeton: The Kingston Press, Inc., 1985), 179-186. Between 1941 and 1945, Nazi Germany and its collaborators carried out the Holocaust, resulting in the murder of six million Jews and five million others. See Martin Gilbert, *The Holocaust: A History of the Jews of Europe During the Second World War* (New York: Holt, Reinhart and Winston, 1985), 824.

99   The wedding dress was not bought but borrowed from Marguerite Mansour who had almost exact dimensions and who got married a few weeks earlier.

100   An Arab Greek Orthodox priest officiating at holy matrimony at a Lutheran institution was unusual in those days but it did happen.

5. Our Neighborhood, 1940s

101   Save the Greek Compound, "A Paleolithic Connection," http://www.savethegreekcompound.com/connections/.

102   Save the Greek Compound, "The Canaanite Connection," ibid.

103   Amir Eshel, *Futurity: Contemporary Literature and the Quest for the Past* (Chicago: The University of Chicago Press, 2013), 164.

104   Times of Israel Staff, "Luxury complex threatens ancient site on Jerusalem's Hill of Evil Counsel," *The Times of Israel* (March 14, 2016), http://www.timesofisrael.com/luxury-complex-threatens-ancient-site-on-jerusalems-hill-of-evil-counsel/.

105   See Save the Greek Compound, "The Christian Connection," ibid., and Don Nissenbaum, *A Street Divided: Stories from Jerusalem's Alley of God*, ibid., 40-43.

106   Two main narratives present themselves. Matthew 27:3-10 states, "When Judas, his betrayer, saw that Jesus was condemned, he repented and brought back the thirty pieces of silver to the chief priests and the elders. He said, 'I have sinned by betraying innocent blood.' But they said, 'What is that to us? See to it yourself.' Throwing down the pieces of silver in the temple, he departed; and he went and hanged himself. But the chief priests, taking

the pieces of silver said, 'It is not lawful to put them into the treasury, since they are blood money.' After conferring together, they used them to buy the potter's field as a place to bury foreigners. For this reason that field has been called the Field of Blood to this day." In contrast, the Acts of the Apostles (1:18-19) says that Judas "acquired a field with the reward of his wickedness; and falling headlong, he burst open in the middle and all of his bowels gushed out. This became known to all the residents of Jerusalem, so that the field was called in their language Hakeldama, that is, Field of Blood."

107 Don Nissenbaum, *A Street Divided: Stories from Jerusalem's Alley of God*, ibid., 41.

108 Henry William Bartlett, *Walks about the City and Environs of Jerusalem* (London: George Virtue, 1844), 60-61.

109 Colonel Sir Charles W. Wilson, with an Introduction by Zev Vilnay, *Jerusalem: The Holy City* (Jerusalem: Ariel Publishing House, n.d.), 73.

110 Ibid., 110.

111 Yosef Navon, born in Jerusalem in 1858, is a Sephardic Jew who distinguished himself as a businessman and is credited with securing the permit from the Ottoman authorities to build the Jaffa-Jerusalem railway. Another accomplishment is the founding of the Mahne Yehuda neighborhood. He died in France in 1934.

112 Don Nissenbaum, *A Street Divided: Stories from Jerusalem's Alley of God*, ibid., 43.

113 Rochelle Davis, "The Growth of the Western Communities, 1917-1948," in Salim Tamari, ed., *Jerusalem 1948: The Arab Neighborhoods and their Fate in the War* (Jerusalem: The Institute of Jerusalem Studies and Bethlehem: Badil Resource Center, 1999), 56.

114 *Aelia* or *Illiya* is a 7th-century Arab Muslim name for Jerusalem. The name's origin is *Aelia Capitolina*, the official name of Jerusalem under the Romans.

115 These are probably the same blockhouses where the dozen or so Jewish families lived between the late 1880s and the late 1920s.

116 Hebron is revered by Jews, Christians, and Muslims, and is considered sacred by Jews and Muslims. The holy site in it, known to Muslims as the Sanctuary of Abraham, and to Jews as the Cave of the Patriarchs (and Matriarchs), contains the double tombs of Abraham and Sarah, Isaac and Rebecca, and Jacob and Leah.

117 Kimberly Katz, translator, annotator, introducer, *A Young Palestinian's Diary, 1941-1945: The Life of Sami ʿAmer*, ibid., 10.

118 Salim Tamari and Issam Nassar, eds., *The Storyteller of Jerusalem: The Life and Times of Wasif Jawhariyyeh, 1904-1948*, ibid., 231.

119 Kimberly Katz, *A Young Palestinian's Diary, 1941-1945: The Life of Sami ʿAmer*, ibid., 82. See also ʿArif al-ʿArif, *Al-Mufassal fi taʾrikh al-Quds* (A Detailed History of Jerusalem), 5th ed. (Jerusalem: Matbʿat al-Maʿarif, 1999), 466, for a listing of prices in Palestine during this period.

120 It is believed that Tatiana eventually lived in Romema, a neighborhood in northwest Jerusalem and frequented the Gorny Convent in Ein Karem, also in southwest Jerusalem, some 4.7 miles (7.6 km) away. Both areas were located within Israel between 1948 and 1967. Gorny, meaning mountainous in Russian, has three churches, a nunnery, a pilgrims hostel, and a cemetery, all situated within a compound wall. Ein Karem means "Spring of the Vineyard" in Arabic and is considered the birthplace of John the Baptist, the son of Elizabeth who is the cousin of Mary, Jesus's mother.

121 See the different scenes that occur when a boy is born as opposed to when a girl is born in Geoffrey Furlonge, *Palestine Is My Country: The Story of Musa Alami* (New York: Praeger Publishers, 1969), 4-6.

6. War, 1948

122 The British Mandate for Palestine, arrived at the meeting of the Supreme Council of the League of Nations in San Remo, Italy, on April 25, 1920, was formally approved by the League of Nations on July 24, 1922, and became effective on September 29, 1923.

123 Bernard Wasserstein, *Divided Jerusalem: The Struggle for the Holy City*, ibid., 82.

124 Samih K. Farsoun and Naseer H. Aruri, *Palestine and the Palestinians: A Social and Political History*, ibid., 93. See also Salim Tamari, "The City and its Rural Hinterland," in SalimTamari, ed. *Jerusalem 1948: The Arab Neighbourhoods and their Fate in the War*, ibid., 81; and Bernard Wasserstein, *Divided Jerusalem: The Struggle for the Holy City*, ibid., 145.

125 Ibid.

126 Issa J. Boullata, *The Bells of Memory: A Palestinian Boyhood in Jerusalem*, ibid., 74.

127 United Nations, Resolution adopted on the Report of the Ad Hoc Committee on the Palestinian Question, 181 (II) Future Government of Palestine," https://documents-dds-ny.un.org/RESOLUTION/GEN/NR0/038/88/IMG/NR03888.PDF?OpenElement.

128 See UNRWA, "Palestine Refugees," http://www.unrwa.org/ palestine-refugees.

129 Wasif Jawhariyyeh in Salim Tamari and Issam Nassar, eds., *The Storyteller of Jerusalem: The Life and Times of Wasif Jawhariyyeh, 1904-1948*, ibid., 242.

130 Hala Sakakini, *Jerusalem and I, A Personal Record*, ibid., 110.
131 Betty Dagher Majaj, *A War Without Chocolate: One Woman's Journey Through Two Nations, Three Wars, and Four Children* (Middletown, DE: np, 2015), 89-90.
132 Issa J. Boullata, *The Bells of Memory*, Ibid., 75-76.
133 Ibid., 75.
134 Quoted in Yair Sheleg, "A Short History of Terror," *Haaretz* (December 3, 2001), http://www.haaretz.com/print-edition/features/ a-short-history-of-terror-1.76345.
135 "Civil War in Palestine: November 29, 1947-May 15, 1948," http://www.zionism-israel.cm/his/Israel_war_ independence_ 1948_timeline.htm.
136 Pat McDonnell Twair, "The Children of Deir Yassin," http://www.deiryassin.org/orphanshome.html.
137 Nathan Krystall, "The Fall of the New City 1947-1950," in SalimTamari, ed. *Jerusalem 1948*, ibid., 108.
138 Constantine X. Mavrides became the father-in-law of my aunt Leila Korfiatis when she was married to his son Elia Mavrides.
139 See Appendix I, "War in the Old City: The Diaries of Constantine Mavrides, May 15-December 30, 1948", in SalimTamari, ed. *Jerusalem 1948*, ibid., 263-264.
140 Jacob J. Nammar, *Born in Jerusalem, Born Palestinian: A Memoir* (Northampton, MA: Olive Branch Press, Interlink Publishing Group, Inc., 2012), 61.
141 Frosso and Farah Abu Jaber are the parents of Kamel S. Abu Jaber, former Jordanian Senator, Minister of Foreign Affairs, 1991-93, and Emeritus Professor of Political Science at the University of Jordan.
142 Terry Rempel, "Dispossession and Restitution in 1948 Jerusalem," in SalimTamari, ed. *Jerusalem 1948*, ibid., 213, 216-217.
143 UNRWA, "Where We Work", http://www.unrwa.org/where-we-work/.
144 Nazmi Juʿbeh, "Focus: Jewish Settlement in the Old City of Jerusalem after 1967," *Palestine-Israel Journal* 8, 1 (2001), http://www.pij.org/details.php?id=166.
145 United Nations, "Resolutions adopted by the General Assembly during its Third Session," http://un.org/documents/ga/res/3/ ares3.htm.
146 See Appendix I, "War in the Old City: The Diaries of Constantine Mavrides," ibid., 263.
147 Wasif Jawhariyyeh in Salim Tamari and Issam Nassar, eds., *The Storyteller of Jerusalem: The Life and Times of Wasif Jawhariyyeh, 1904-1948*, ibid., 255.
148 Don Nissenbaum, *A Street Divided: Stories from Jerusalem's Alley of God*, ibid., 17.

149   Ibid., 121. See also Benny Morris, *The Birth of the Palestinian Refugee Problem, 1947-1949* (Cambridge: Cambridge University Press, 1987), 193.
150   Arnon Golan, ibid., 131.
151   Following all kinds of Jordanian-Palestinian maneuvering, King Abdullah of Jordan wanted to strengthen his presence in Jerusalem and the West Bank. In a Palestine Arab Congress that was held in Jericho on December 1, 1948 (the week after my family left Jericho and a day after Dayan and El-Tell carved up of Jerusalem), with the backing of Palestinian leaders from Hebron and Nablus, he was proclaimed King of Palestine. The union of the West Bank, including East Jerusalem, and the East Bank was ratified by the Jordanian Parliament on April 24, 1950. As for the Gaza Strip, it remained under the direct or indirect control of Egypt between 1948 and 1967.

7. Our Neighborhood, 1950-2000

152   Don Nissenbaum, *A Street Divided: Stories from Jerusalem's Alley of God*, ibid., 19.
153   Bernard Wasserstein, *Divided Jerusalem: The Struggle for the Holy City*, 2nd Ed., ibid., 180.
154   Raphael Israeli, *Jerusalem Divided: The Armistice Regime, 1947-1967* (London and New York: Routledge, 2013), 131.
155   This is part of the Palestinian narrative related to the years of homelessness and despair, as provided in Sami ʿAdwan, Dan Bar-On, and Eyal Naveh, eds., PRIME Peace Research Institute in the Middle East, *Side By Side: Parallel Histories of Israel-Palestine*, ibid., 147.
156   The assassin, Mustapha Shukri Ashu, was a member of the Arab Dynamite Squad, part of the irregular forces that were associated with Hajj Amin and engaged in the Arab-Jewish fighting during Mandated Palestine. See "Assassination of King Abdullah," *The Guardian*, July 21, 1951, www.theguardian.com/theguardian/ 1951/jul/21/fromthearchive.
157   Charles D. Smith, *Palestine and the Arab-Israeli Conflict*, 3rd Ed. (New York: St. Martin's Press, Inc., 1996), 244.
158   Bernard Wasserstein, *Divided Jerusalem*, ibid., 189.
159   *Talamiz* is the plural of *tilmiz* and *tullab* is the plural of *talib*.
160   In 1949, the population in West Jerusalem was estimated at 69,000, with only 931 Christians and 28 Muslims. See Meron Benvenisti and Editorial Staff, "The Divided City (1948-1967)," in *Jerusalem* (Jerusalem: Keter Publishing House, Ltd., 1973), 170.
161   For a good summary of the finding of the Cross, see William Saunders, "St. Helena and the True Cross," *Arlington Catholic Herald* (October

15, 2014): http://www.catholicherald.com/stories/ Finding-of-the-true-cross,27329.
162 UNRWA. http://www.unrwa.org.
163 In those days, the lines were drawn in religious cement. My father-in-law, Stephan Yaᶜcoub Zakharia, a Greek Orthodox Christian, and my mother-in-law, Munira Tawfiq Bayyouk, a Roman Catholic, were married at the Melkite Greek Catholic Church, an Eastern Catholic Church in full communion with the Holy See. Their individual churches would not marry them unless their spouse-to-be was or became of the same denomination.
164 St. Onuphrius lived in the Egyptian desert during the 3rd or 4th century AD and is always depicted in icons as an old, slender hermit with long hair, a long beard, and leaves as loincloth.
165 Gilbert, 1996, p. 2.
166 Hanan ᶜAshrawi, *This Side of Peace: A Personal Account* (New York: Simon & Schuster, 1995), 35.
167 A similar scene is described by Wasif Jawhariyyeh in Salim Tamari and Issam Nassar, eds., *The Storyteller of Jerusalem: The Life and Times of Wasif Jawhariyyeh, 1904-1948*, ibid., 59.
168 Christians in Jerusalem, like many elsewhere, usually frown upon other Christians marrying outside their religion. In Muslim Arab culture, however, it is taboo for a Muslim woman to marry a non-Muslim man unless he converts to Islam or for a Muslim man to convert to another religion so as to marry a woman from that religion. But, it is allowed for a Muslim man to marry a woman who belongs to "People of the Book," that is, Jewish and Christian. This is true even though the Qur'an specifies that Muslims may marry believers in any other religion as long as they believe in God's Oneness and do not attribute partners to Him. See Qur'an 2:221; 2:62; 60:10. Moreover, in Arab culture, as in several other cultures around the world, girls and women take their lives into their own hands when they act in a way contrary to their family's dictates or red lines. As Human Rights Watch explains, "Honor killings are acts of vengeance, usually death, committed by male family members against female family members, who are held to have brought dishonor upon the family…The mere perception that a woman has behaved in a way that "dishonors" her family is sufficient to trigger an attack on her life". Human Rights Watch, "Violence Against Women and 'Honor' Crimes," https://www.hrw.org/legacy/press/ 2001/04/un_oral12_0405.htm.
169 Israel studied painting at the Avni Institute in Tel Aviv. He did his post-graduate studies at the Hornsey College of Art in London, England. After teaching sculpture and design at Bezalel Academy of Art in Jerusalem, he exhibited in many individual and group shows in Israel and elsewhere

around the world and has a variety of public works, also in Israel and beyond. He is the recipient of Israeli and international awards and prizes, and is considered among the top of Israel's artists. See Israel Hadany, *Visual Memories* (Israel: The Open Museum Industrial Parks Tefen and Omer, 2003-2004) and Israel Hadany, *Spirit Constructions—Israel Hadany: The Quest for the Sacred* (Israel: Beit Avi Chai, 2010).

8. Our Neighbors, Our Friends

170 A survey of two housing blocks (#30018 and #30019) found 193 parcels containing 101 houses, all owned by Arab families. Among the 50 families mentioned are Christian, including Kattan, Al Munayyer, Semonian, and Zahra, and Muslim, including Abu Al-Feelat, Abu Khater, Alami, Al-Tori, Barakat, Dahoodi, Hashemee, Nashashebeh, Al Qar'een, Shwaikeh, and Sultan. See Adnan Abdelrazek, *The Arab Architectural Renaissance in the Western Part of Occupied Jerusalem*, published in Arabic under the auspices of the Arab Studies Society (Jerusalem: Manar Press, 2010), 66, and in English (Cyprus: Rimal Books, 2017), 92.

171 Bimkom, "Survey of Palestinian Neighborhoods in East Jerusalem: Abu-Thor," http://www.bimkom.org/eng/wp-content/uploads/2.10_abu-Thor-w.pdf.

172 Rabbi Daniel Landes, "Jerusalem Coexistence?: Violence is the New Normal in Abu Tor," ibid.

173 Noah Browning, "Palestinian anger boils in the heart of East Jerusalem," ibid.

174 Daniel K. Eisenbud, "Seven Arabs arrested for attacking Jews on Jerusalem promenade," The Jerusalem Post (July 29, 2015), http://m.jpost.com/Arab-Israeli-Conflict/Seven-Arabs-arrested-for-attacking-Jews-on-Jerusalem-promenade-410556#article=6018RjlwMD15NkE115NEFCRjRCNEEyRTk2MTk2MTQ5MJlGHzk=.

175 See Judy Maltz, "Arabs and Jews Join Forces to Oppose Development on Historic Jerusalem Hilltop," *Haaretz* (February 17, 2016), http://www.haaretz.com/israel-news/.premium-1.703933; Times of Israel Staff, "Luxury complex threatens ancient site on Jerusalem's Hill of Evil Counsel," *The Times of Israel* (March 14, 2016), http://timesofisrael.com/luxury-complex-threatens-ancient-site-on-jerusalems-hill-of-evil-counsel/; and Joshua Mitnick, "Reaching Across the Seam Line," *The New York Jewish Week* (May 17, 2017), http://jewishweek.timesofisrael.com/reaching-across-the-seam-line.

9. Family Profiles

176 George Antonius, *The Arab Awakening: The Story of the Arab National Movement* (London: Hamish Hamilton, 1938).

177 The Catholic Church began saying mass in the vernacular languages, like Arabic, at the end of November 1964 and stopped using Latin altogether as the liturgical language in 1969.

178 The profile of my sister Anastasia takes excerpts from Saliba Sarsar, "Witnessing in Jerusalem: A Loving Tribute to Sister Anastas Sarsar," Catholic News Agency, June 19, 2014, http://www.catholicnewsagency.com/column/witnessing-in-jerusalem-a-loving-tribute-to-sister-anastas-sarsar-2918/.

179 Pope Francis, "Visit at the Homeless Shelter "Dono Di Maria": Meeting with the Missionaries of Charity," May 21, 2013, http://m.vatican.va/content/framcescomobile/en/speeches/2013/may/documents/papa-francesco_20130521_dono-di-maria.html.

180 Issa J. Boullata, *The Bells of Memory*, ibid., 57.

181 The Majali family has been close to the Hashemite Royal Family. Hazza^c Barakat al-Majali was twice Prime Minister of Jordan. The second time ended when he was assassinated in his office along with other senior government officials on August 29, 1960. Ayman Hazza^c Majali was Chief of the Royal Protocol for King Hussein, Deputy Prime Minister under King Abdullah II, and a member of the Jordanian Parliament. Amjad served as Jordanian Ambassador to Bahrain and Greece and then Minister of Labor in Jordan.

182 Yaalo was depopulated of its Palestinian inhabitants and destroyed, along with Beit Nuba and Imwas, by the Israel Defense Forces during the June 1967 War. Canada Park, also known as Ayalon Park, extends over its territory. The Jarallah family lost much there, with flat big acreage of land, a house, an artesian well, a pool, and a tractor. Less than a year later, the huge lot in the plain was fenced and planted by an Israeli food company.

183 In Halhoul, a Palestinian city located 5 kilometers north of Hebron, the Jarallah family lost a rich agricultural property situated on a high elevation, terraced, with a tremendous vineyard, pine trees, and a stone oven for grilling. It is now part of an Israeli settlement.

184 Nusseibeh was a leading Palestinian personality and public servant in the Arab national movement and Palestinian affairs. He held numerous posts during the British Mandate and in the Jordanian Government, including Minister of Defense, Minister of Development and Reconstruction, Minister of Interior, Minister of Education, Governor of Jerusalem, and Ambassador to the Court of St. James.

AUTHOR'S BIOGRAPHY

Saliba Sarsar, born and raised in Jerusalem, is Professor of Political Science at Monmouth University. His B.A. in political science and history interdisciplinary, summa cum laude, is from Monmouth College, and his Ph.D. in political science is from Rutgers University. He is the author and co-author of numerous books, articles, and commentaries; co-editor of *Patriarch Michel Sabbah—Faithful Witness: On Reconciliation and Peace in the Holy Land*; and editor of *What Jerusalem Means to Us: Christian Perspectives and Reflections*. He has three books of poetry: *Crosswinds*, *Seven Gates of Jerusalem*, and *Portraits: Poems of the Holy Land*. He was featured in *The New York Times*, "His Mission: Finding Why People Fight—A Witness to Mideast Conflict Turns to Dialogue and Peace." Among his honors are the Award of Academic Excellence from the American Task Force on Palestine, Holy Land Christian Ecumenical Foundation Award, *Global Visionary Award* and *Stafford Presidential Award of Excellence* from Monmouth University, and *Humanitarian Award* from the National Conference for Community and Justice.

www.ingramcontent.com/pod-product-compliance
Lightning Source LLC
Chambersburg PA
CBHW052022070526
44584CB00016B/1857